speaking in tongues

speaking in tongues

BY H. J. STOLEE

OMNIA VINCIT VERITAS

Augsburg Publishing House
Minneapolis, Minnesota

SPEAKING IN TONGUES

This volume is a reprint of *Pentecostalism*, The Problem of the
Modern Tongues Movement, copyright 1936 by Augsburg
Publishing House.

INTRODUCTION

WHEN Dr. Stolee wrote his book on "The Problem of the Modern Tongues Movement," of which this volume is a reprint, the title he chose, *Pentecostalism,* was accurate. The phenomenon known as "speaking in tongues" was generally considered a characteristic of certain sects, notably those which went by the name "Pentecostal," using the term more in the generic than in the specific sense.

In the minds of most people there was more than a taint of fanaticism clinging to the practice of speaking in tongues. It might not be considered quite in the same category as the "snake-handling" which characterizes certain fringe-sects in the Deep South. Nevertheless, there was a vast difference between the phenomenon of speaking in tongues and the manifestations of the Spirit usually found in the historic churches of Protestantism. Dr. Stolee's book reflects accurately the traditional characteristics of speaking in tongues and the attitude of most Protestants toward it.

The late '50s and early '60s of the twentieth century have witnessed a significant change in attitude toward the tongues movement. It is this fact which justifies the reprint of a book written 36 years ago.

There are those who contend that there is less emphasis today on speaking in tongues in the sects which, historically, have been the chief proponents of the phenomenon than there was formerly. This is a contention which it would be impossible to prove or disprove statistically. To whatever extent the observation is true, this lessening of emphasis is probably accounted for by the fact that as a sect becomes more firmly established, it tends to take upon itself more and more of the characteristics of the historic churches, with a consequent lessening of emphasis on the peculiarities which caused it to be formed and which were the sources of its early growth.

On the other hand, today we find some within the historic churches who have become deeply interested in the tongues movement and claim to find in it a special manifestation of the Holy Spirit. Not least is this true of a number, both lay and clergy, within the liturgical churches of Protestantism, Lutherans and Episcopalians. Existing in this more intellectual and sophisticated atmosphere, a more rational theology of speaking in tongues seems in the process of formulation. An effort is being made to demonstrate that this phenomenon fulfills rather than negates the theology of the historic churches. Even the term used to describe it has taken on a more sophisticated ring: today it is "glossalalia" rather than "speaking in tongues."

Nevertheless, basically there is no discernible difference between these newer manifestations of speaking in tongues and those described by Dr. Stolee. The dress may be more modern and the framework more sophisticated in the parish hall of some Lutheran or Episcopal church than in some store-front meeting house. Despite that, the traditional sectarian setting differs little from that which has now developed in the historic churches.

When one faces the question, "Why has glossalalia moved from the store-front to the church?" one is confronted with many and varied, and sometimes contradictory, views.

By and large, however, here also one finds only a few opinions which are new. Its proponents speak of it as a gift of the Holy Spirit. Many consider it as being inseparably linked with "baptism of the Holy Spirit." It is held to be "part of the equipment of the church" in her task of witness. Nothing new here.

On the other hand, not a few voices are raised which attempt to account for the spread of speaking in tongues in the historic churches by pointing to the weaknesses of those churches. Some compare it with the liturgical movement and state that, just as the liturgical movement aims to fulfill the worship of the church, so does speaking in tongues. Its critics state that the interest being displayed in speaking in tongues results from a doubt in the minds of its proponents as to the complete sufficiency of the revealed Means of Grace, Word and Sacraments. Others maintain that, at least as far as clergymen are concerned, it is because their theological foundations are not secure that they attempt to find security in this special gift of the Spirit.

Whatever the causes, there is little doubt but that the result is tension. And disquiet, too. A number of studies by properly constituted groups within the churches have raised serious questions as to the dangers inherent in the tongues movement. One "study document," not yet made public property, lists, among other points, rather critical, the following: There is a tendency to bring pressure on people that they may "receive" the gift and to be critical of those who do not so "receive." There is actually nothing in this phenomenon which is not already given through use of Word and Sacraments.

Another study shares in the concerns of the one alluded to, but adds in much more amicable terms "that Christians who believe that they have experienced 'speaking in tongues' or 'ecstatic utterance' are not to be forbidden to do so. . . ."

Dr. Stolee's book is reprinted at this time in the hope that its scriptural approach to a difficult subject and its irenic spirit may serve to keep the discussion of speaking in tongues in proper perspective and even lead to a God-pleasing understanding of the true meaning of fullness of the Spirit in the hearts of men and in the life of the church.

O. G. MALMIN

CONTENTS

Come, Holy Spirit, heavenly Dove,
With all Thy quickening powers,
And light a flame of sacred love
In these cold hearts of ours.

See how we grovel here below,
Fond of these trifling toys;
Our souls, how heavily they go
To reach eternal joys.

In vain we tune our lifeless songs,
In vain we strive to rise;
Hosannas languish on our tongues,
And our devotion dies.

Come, Holy Spirit, heavenly Dove,
With all Thy quickening powers;
Come, shed abroad a Savior's love,
And that shall kindle ours. Amen.

(Isaac Watts)

RELIGIOUS MOVEMENTS

The coming of such movements.
The heart's longing for rest.
The soul seeking expression.
Growth in Grace.

Watchman, what of the night? Watchman, what of the night? The watchman said, The morning cometh, and also the night: if ye will inquire, inquire ye: turn ye, come (Isaiah 21:11, 12).

Then said he unto me, Prophesy unto the wind, prophesy, son of man, and say to the wind, Thus saith the Lord Jehovah: Come from four winds, O breath, and breathe upon these slain, that they may live (Ezekiel 37:9).

The wind bloweth where it will, and thou hearest the voice thereof, but knowest not whence it cometh, and whither it goeth: so is every one that is born of the Spirit (John 3:8).

When Jehovah brought back those that returned to Zion, We were like unto them that dream. Then was our mouth filled with laughter, And our tongue with singing: Then said they among the nations, Jehovah hath done great things for them. Jehovah hath done great things for us, Whereof we are glad. Turn again our captivity, O Jehovah, As the streams in the South (Psalm 126:1-4).

Come unto me, all ye that labor and are heavy laden, and I will give you rest. Take my yoke upon you, and learn of me; for I am meek and lowly in heart: and ye shall find rest unto your souls (Matt. 11:28, 29).

As newborn babes, long for the spiritual milk which is without guile, that ye may grow thereby unto salvation; if ye have tasted that the Lord is gracious (1 Peter 2:2, 3).

But if the watchman see the sword come, and blow not the trumpet, and the people be not warned, and the sword come, and take any person from among them; he is taken away in his iniquity, but his blood will I require at the watchman's hand (Ezek. 33:6).

CHAPTER ONE

Religious Movements

RELIGIOUS movements ebb and flow in every era of the Church. Sometimes to the proportions of tidal waves. At times the tide of spiritual manifestations seem to move in the same direction as do the external and established activities of Church life. At other times the current tends toward the very opposite of regular and regulated effort.

In some generations the extraordinary may trace its origin directly to the vigorous spiritual life of believers, while in other periods the religious movements apparently are the reaction to apathy or to paralysis within the organized congregations.

Whenever a religious, or more correctly, spiritual, movement advances to such an extent that the unbelievers as well as the believers are stirred thereby, the situation demands especial attention. If it takes on the proportions of a mass movement many kinds of by-products may appear. Some of these are the welcome signs of a new vigor; others have the appearance of unsound stimulation.

Whether the religious movement appears as the rapid growth of spring time, or as the urgent in-gathering of harvest, a large measure of the grace and knowledge of the Lord Jesus Christ is required to enable us to work effectually. Weeds thrive even when a cold spring retards the tender seedlings. Also, it is extremely difficult to keep all tares out of the sheaves when summer heat necessitates a reaping early and late.

Nevertheless, "he that observeth the wind shall not

sow; and he that regardeth the clouds shall not reap."
Whenever we are confronted with problems we also are
facing possibilities. Possibilities, it is true, for good or for
evil in the Church. It may be a most heartening sign of
the Holy Spirit's quickening power in our midst. On the
other hand it may be the counterfeit manifestations of a
spirit which is not of God.

Therefore all serious minded Christians, and particularly those who are set to be "watchmen on the walls of
Zion" can not and will not lightly approve or disapprove.
They will pray for grace to discern, and then in the light
of the revealed Word prove the spirits, whether they be
of God.

The true pastor will exercise care not to quell every
spirit lest he also quench the Spirit from God, and "be
found even to be fighting against God" (Acts 5:39). He
will not with an air of superiority ignore every "sound
of marching in the tops of the mulberry trees." Though
at first like a mere breath of air, it may be the time to
bestir himself, for perchance then is the Lord gone out
to smite the enemy.

Religious upheavals, be they sound or unsound, ought
not to be dismissed from one's mind with the indolent
observation that "history repeats itself." For in this respect history is as much a lesson of warning as it is of
consolation. Men are slow to heed the experiences of
the past. He who is to lead God's people forward that
they may take possession of the spiritual heritage awaiting
them, needs to recall the words: "Ye have not passed this
way heretofore" (Josh. 3:4). Intellectual power and
years of experience are not sufficient, for the crossing
of such a "Jordan." The safe and Scriptural way is to
"follow the ark."

The regular, work-a-day routine in the Lord's vineyard,
of both men and of women, requires a constant, daily

refreshing and directing from the Word. That is the Holy Spirit's method and means. Otherwise there will be "program minus power." The life of the individual and of the group will stagnate and petrify, "having a form of godliness, but denying the power thereof."

Likewise the only effective and defensible procedure in dealing with extraordinary spiritual situations is a diligent and yielded heeding of how Christ and the apostles applied the promises as well as the judgments of the Word to men who in puzzle or in panic asked: "What meaneth this?" If the spiritual leader assumes the role of a dictator, ready to attack and to crush every movement of which he himself was not the originator, the outcome usually is an open break and straying into error and fanaticism on the part of some, and the smothering of the weak spiritual flame in others, leaving them more cold and lifeless than ever.

In our efforts to reach impenitent souls we are tempted to turn to a form of preaching which is strongly emotional. As Dr. Hallesby puts it, "By sad stories and other kinds of sentimentality they appealed to the unregenerate man's purely natural religious emotions. And when these emotions had been brought to the melting point, the preacher would try in good faith to weld them together with faith in the free grace of God. But naturally this welding gave way under the impact of the very first strain that it encountered."

Religious movements usually cause awakenings, but not always genuine conversions. This is especially true of the great mass-revivals in the Church. The result of the "altar-call" has too often been a perennial stir and subsequent back-sliding. However, it should be clear to all that such need not necessarily be the fruitage. Thank God, there are thousands of God's people that have been brought to faith, or restored to faith in such revivals, and have remained firm and consecrated in the true faith.

Let it be said too, that *believers* need to be quickened. There is little of God-pleasing enthusiasm in us. We need to be revived by the Spirit's gracious ministry through the Word for we so easily have a relapse into compromise and worldliness. And when such is the case we hinder others from being attracted to the Church and to the Church's Lord.

That does not mean that men are to be attracted primarily to the teacher, the preacher, or the evangelist. "Cursed is the man that trusteth in man." But there is a desirable influence to be wielded by anyone who speaks "as the Word of God." "I am certain that this influence is in accordance with the will of the Lord and is a part of God's plan for the salvation of the individual. It is true that it is possible for this influence to emanate only from the spirit of man, in which event the results also will only be human. But this should not be allowed to blind us to the fact that the Spirit of God does not make use only of men's words, but also of their wills and their feelings, as means of exercising a saving influence upon others. The influence which both audience and preacher exert upon an individual affects both his conscious and his subconscious soul-life." (Hallesby.)

In a lecture to future church leaders, a Christian physician says: "We live in an age when religious longing is strong enough, but does not always turn toward the Church. What is the reason of this? Is it not that the Church does not always turn toward the religious longing? It does not try to regard each individual human being according to his or her individual character and capacity, with all peculiarities of psychic structure. The Church has often endeavored to put people into a definite spiritual uniform; but people nowadays will not wear uniforms. They cannot and will not adapt themselves to anything of the sort. They must be themselves also in their religious life. And they have the right."

In the hearts of those who know not Christ there are often strange, unexpressed longings for something higher and nobler in life. There is a feeling of emptiness in existence, a consciousness of sin, a wish—though not yet a will —to find God. There is a sense of the winsomeness of Jesus and a wistful looking to those who profess to be His followers.

It is just such God-given dissatisfaction that must not be confused with the erratic desires and attitudes of fanatics or men who refuse to be directed and refreshed by the Word of God. There should be a holy purpose in the heart of every disciple not only to "press on" but also "to lay hold on," to reach out for, and to secure that Christ-likeness, that holiness without which no man shall see the Lord.

There is union between a believing soul and God. It is a mystical union, but it does not imply a mystifying behavior or a mysterious existence. It is mystical because it is spiritual and intimate beyond human understanding.

The Holy Spirit is both cause and effect of this union with Christ, for the Spirit dwells in the heart. It is a union that is not to remain barren; it causes us to bear fruit, more fruit, much fruit.

It is true that one may perhaps be a Christian with but a faint consciousness of the presence of the Holy Spirit in the soul. Even at best such a spiritual condition is an unsatisfactory, unhappy experience and usually means that the work of the Spirit is being hindered somewhere.

The Church needs the vitality, the eagerness, the religious fire, and the singleness of heart that marks healthy youth. This is true when we think of the young in faith, the youth in Christ, as well as young in years. Young life must grow. Growth refers not only to stature but also to sound firmness of form and frame; a firmness that enables men to bear the burdens of the day.

It is better that men be "babes in Christ" than that they be lifeless corpses. But babes need wholesome food and patient care. Parents do not cuff and kick a babe who stumbles and falls while learning to walk. Yes, even a sick or crippled child is still a child. It requires much love and patience and skill to bring such a one up to be "a full-grown man, unto the measure of the stature of the fulness of Christ."

This takes more than a day, it takes more than a year, but by the grace of God babes do grow to beautiful and useful manhood and womanhood. Then they are "no longer children, tossed to and fro and carried about with every wind of doctrine, by the sleight of men, in craftiness, after the wiles of error, but speaking the truth in love, may grow up in all things into him, who is the head, even Christ."

THE KIN OF PENTECOSTALISM

Not a new movement.

Speaking in Tongues.

The old record of the Tongues Movement.

The Montanist prophets.

Other kindred phenomena.

Pentecostals of the Middle Ages.

Such movements among the heathen.

Mohammedan Dervishes.

And the king of Israel said to Jehoshaphat, Did I not tell thee that he would not prophesy good concerning me, but evil? And Micaiah said, Therefore hear thou the word of Jehovah: I saw Jehovah sitting on his throne, and all the host of heaven standing by him on his right hand and on his left. And Jehovah said, Who shall entice Ahab, that he may go up and fall at Ramothgilead? And one said on this manner; and another said on that manner. And there came forth a spirit, and stood before Jehovah, and said, I will entice him. And Jehovah said unto him, Wherewith? And he said, I will go forth, and will be a lying spirit in the mouth of all his prophets. And he said, Thou shalt entice him, and shalt prevail also: go forth, and do so. Now therefore, behold, Jehovah hath put a lying spirit in the mouth of all these thy prophets; and Jehovah hath spoken evil concerning thee (1 Kings 22:18-23).

But there arose false prophets also among the people, as among you also there shall be false teachers, who shall privily bring in destructive heresies, denying even the Master that bought them, bringing upon themselves swift destruction. And many shall follow their lascivious doings; by reason of whom the way of the truth shall be evil spoken of (2 Peter 2:1-3).

Let no man rob you of your prize by a voluntary humility and worshipping of the angels, dwelling in the things which he hath not seen, vainly puffed up by his fleshly mind, and not holding fast the Head, from whom all the body, being supplied and knit together through the joints and bands, increaseth with the increase of God (Col. 2:18, 19).

CHAPTER TWO

The Kin of Pentecostalism

PERPLEXITIES and problems were not wanting even in the apostolic churches. There were errors in doctrine and inconsistencies in practice. The Christians needed reproof and correction and instruction in righteousness. This very fact has been turned to good for the Church in all generations following. The Holy Spirit who illumined and directed the apostles in the planting and watering of the Early Church, caused the epistles to be written wherein are described the symptoms, the cause and cure of all spiritual ailments and abnormalities in congregations and in individuals.

Whether in the letters of James or Peter or Paul or John we find that where the doctrine was wrong in any place, it would soon be reflected also in wrong practice. There is nothing new under the sun, not even in sects or cults. Practically all modern "isms" and religious vagaries can be traced to some ancient heresy with which the apostles or their immediate successors had to contend. Modernists are not modern. The "New Thought" of numerous twentieth century prophets is the same philosophy and vain deceit that threatened to make spoil of the saints in the first century.

Modern pentecostalism also has its type in the problems of the early Church. Its ancestry is most clearly traced to Corinth. We may say without hesitation that the predominating traits in the Corinthian congregation are strikingly similar to the most conspicuous features of the pentecostal churches today.

The name "Pentecostal" is the common denominator applied to several separate sects. Properly used, this designation is not a reflection on anyone, and many desire to be known by this name. In fact, some communions include the word "pentecostal" in their official corporate title.

Pentecostal sects are not agreed on all doctrines and practices. But they have certain specific features in common which distinguish them from other denominations. Chief among such features is the teaching that *sanctification reaches its highest plane in a "spirit baptism" manifested in some ecstatic or mystic experience, preferably in the "speaking in tongues."* They assert that the "gift of tongues" in their midst is the same gift and for the same purpose as it was on the day of Pentecost. Hence the name "Pentecostal."

The pentecostalism, however, that we shall discuss in this present writing, is not confined to a few specific sects. It represents an attitude and characteristic as well as a dogma. It is found in a greater or less degree in most communions; indeed even in non-Christian cults.

Pentecostalism finds response in the melancholy introvert who is attracted to mysticism especially when it savors of self-pity. It also appeals to the choleric, high-strung individual. His zeal and his restlessness readily express themselves in a continual seeking for notoriety and spiritual excitement.

The word, "In quietness and in confidence shall be your strength," is a foreign word to the typical pentecostals. Consequently they find it not at all satisfying to rest their souls in the plain statements of Scripture. They would anchor their faith chiefly to subjective experience. They look for the Holy Spirit to make known His ministry to them by some external manifestation, perceptible to the senses rather than received in the heart.

The zenith and finality of pentecostalism is the so-called "tongues movement," that is, the "speaking in tongues" to which we have referred. Anyone who will make even the briefest study of this movement will learn that in the post-apostolic era, in the Middle Ages, and in the Nineteenth Century, the story is much the same. The record is one of ecstasy leading to fanaticism, and then of religious hysteria coupled with gross sensuality.

There has been a persistent tendency to discount the sufficiency of Scripture, and to add or even substitute in its stead the "visions" and "revelations" of their own. Trances and other semi-conscious states are expected. The ravings of insanity have been pitifully common in the wake of the "tongues" movement.

Practically all post-apostolic pentecostalism down to our own time points to the same causes, the same effects, and teach the same moral.

Historic instances of "tongues" are found at intervals. We shall pass by the references in the Bible for the present, because something more than mere mention must be accorded the cases in Acts and First Corinthians. A clear and Spirit-enlightened view of those instances is needed first of all to see God's purpose in those manifestations and then to enable us to prove the spirits that surround us now.

Already in the second century the mystery-mongers and supra-Scripture folk made themselves felt in several churches. A fair specimen is the historically well-known sect, the *Montanists.*

They are named for one Montanus, a native of the table lands of Phrygia. Before his conversion to Christianity he had been a priest of Cybele. The worship of that Oriental goddess was largely divination and clairvoyance, for this section was a hot-bed of superstition. Montanus was a visionary by temperament, and such he remained also after having accepted Christianity. With him, speculation and visions soon supplanted the apostolic epistles and the gospels. He agreed with Persian heathen and Alexandrian Jews concerning the desirability of ecstatic visions.

Particularly do we note that great store was set by the utterances made while in a state of unconsciousness or trance. The "prophetic" utterances thus produced were held to be oracles of God. The individual prophet was not held responsible for the message, even though it be in direct contradiction to the Scriptures. They thus denied Paul's clear statement: "the spirits of the prophets are subject to the prophets." Montanus claimed that the Holy Spirit spoke directly through him. The disciples of Montanus even declared him to be the Paraclete, the Holy Spirit sent in person.

To us the actual behavior of this early sect is of more significance than their philosophies. For by their fruits we shall be able to know whether or not their spiritual descendants are now among us.

Hippolytus (200 A. D.) says of the Montanists: "These are Phrygians by birth, and have been deceived through having been overcome by womenkind ... whom they held for prophetesses, saying that the Comforter Spirit dwelt in them . . . saying that through them (Montanus and the prophetesses) they have learned something more than from the Law and the Prophets and the Gospels. But they glorify these womenkind above apostles." They "invent new fasts and feasts (Col. 2:16-19) and meals of dry food and meals of radishes, saying they were taught them by their womenkind."

Of course this type of exalted, and yet childish, legalism attracted followers. Most of the Church both in the East and West rejected Montanism, though even such men as Tertullian were its spokesmen. Its tenets and practices lingered among the impulsive Gauls for nearly four hundred years. In the days of Montanus, and more especially in later times, many vagaries and immoral practices were charged to the Montanists as the result of their mystic messages.

The "prophetic" phase of Montanism has frequently been repeated in the history of the Church. Perhaps the instances that are of greatest interest to us is the "prophetism" that has occurred several times of late on the mission fields of west Africa.

Of course Africa had its seers long before Christianity touched its soil. Any man who had a vision, or who claimed to speak for the unseen spirits was a prophet. But the so-called "prophetic movement" in west Africa to which we refer is a strange mixture of Christian faith and heathen fetishism exactly as was Montanism of old, and indeed as is fanatic error of all ages. Of the African prophetism we shall have more to say in a subsequent chapter.

Off-shoots of the Montanists were the Priscillians, named for one Priscilla their prophetess who claimed for herself to be inspired. The so-called "Quietists" were another development. Then the "Praying Dancers" of Syria, who instead of being quiet mystics, manifested their spirit as "holy jumpers."

In the fourth century there appeared in Constantinople certain religious phenomena that remind one of the "baptism with tongues" of our day. "Wild, inarticulate cries, words passionate but of little meaning, almost convulsive gestures. . . ." The early records tell us that Bishop Chrysostom met these manifestations with the "sternest possible reproof."

A later tendency had its promoters in the "Pillar Men," the "Stylitiae" of Antioch. They attracted attention for a while during the fifth century. Their technique was to be perched high on pillars in some public place, where men might look up to them as models of spiritual attainment. Traces of this inordinate type of self-exaltation were found in Christendom for about six centuries. It is an example of how the "old man" will thrive on anything that poses as religious self-abasement. (Col. 2:23.)

The Middle Ages of the Church also had their quota of those who, like the Corinthians (1 Cor. 4:6), went "beyond the things which are written." Among these we note that tongues of pentecostalism again come to the fore.

Such spiritual inflation in earlier centuries had been manifested largely in self-publicity of a crude kind, with occasional "utterances" now and then. But European mystics of the Middle Ages were bent on establishing their sanctification more by visions and revelations.

The "Friends of God" of the Rhineland and of Switzerland were "called to superior sanctity . . . and spiritually ruled the community in God's stead . . . Many awful visions were seen by them; many terrible prophecies sent abroad." "They were mystics to the height of mysticism; each member was in direct union with God. . . They had wonders and special revelations."

The "wonders" of the Middle Ages were not limited to metaphysical realms alone. Manifestations of physical effects were by no means wanting. Numerous strange features developed that remind us strongly of the "signs" in present-day pentecostalism.

"In his *Dictionary of Sects,* John Henry speaks of the 'Pastoureaux Movement in Flanders in 1251' and describes a conduct that doubtless would today have been characterized by speaking in tongues." "Of a condition in Amsterdam in 1566, William Howitt in his *History of the Supernatural,* wrote: 'They climbed up the walls and over roofs like cats, made the most horrible grimaces and *spoke in foreign languages* . . . sometimes they became cataleptic, were stiff as trunks of trees, and might be carried about in the same manner'." In England and France similar "speaking in tongues" took place in the same century.

Occasionally someone tells us that Luther claimed for himself "the baptism of tongues." We have never found any authentic writing to verify such an assertion. Whatever in Luther's life that may be referred to, it is certain that he never based his doctrine or practise on any "vision" or "spirit" or "prophet" outside of the Word of God.

In such times of religious upheavals as during the days of Luther one may expect the appearance of a variety of "prophets." The notorious Zwichau prophets are representative of this "school." They claimed to be inspired, and communicated with "the angel Gabriel."

In their arguments with Luther they placed their "special enlightenment" above the Scriptures. "Why cling so closely to the Bible? The Bible! Always the Bible!— It is by the Spirit alone that we can be enlightened. God Himself speaks to us." When Luther answered: "Nothing that you have advanced is based upon Holy Scripture, it is all a mere fable," one of the exasperated zealots shouted, "The spirit, the spirit." To this Luther replied in cool contempt: "I slap your spirit on the snout." The "prophets" found it advisable to leave the community that same day.

In every age there have been church folk who have maintained that if anyone is "very much in earnest," and "sincere about his religion" he should be welcomed as a messenger from God, even though he does not agree with the Scriptures in every message. So also with respect to the "prophets" and "tongue talkers" these nineteen centuries.

We may well grant that this type of people have seldom denied the Scriptural doctrines of atonement in Christ, His resurrection, and His second coming. Their most grave error has been that they would substitute "vision" for faith, psychic experience for growth in grace, and their own unintelligible utterances as superior to the Written Word.

It would be well for anyone interested in such spiritual phenomena whether within or without the pentecostal communions, to notice what Paul refers to when he introduces his chapters concerning spiritual gifts, and more especially the Corinthian "speaking in tongues." He indicates that not every spirit that controls and leads man is from God. "Ye know that when ye were Gentiles, ye were led away unto those dumb idols, *howsoever ye might be led*" (I Cor. 12:2).

In other words, he reminds them of the awful fact that even heathen were spirit-led and spirit-dominated. This, obviously not by God's Holy Spirit. Had the Corinthian Christians witnessed anything in their midst that reminded them of their demon-possessed heathen neighbors?

It cannot be denied that certain rites and actions of the devotees of some pagan cults very strongly resemble the most deplorable traits of "tongues." In pagan Greece there was the Pythia or chief priestess of the Delphian shrine. She generally uttered her messages amid contortions and groans in half-articulate words and mutterings. An "interpreter" was necessary to convey the "inspired message" to ordinary men. Greek mythology also tells how the priestesses of Dionysus during special religious sessions would run about with disheveled hair and frenzied shouts in praise of their idol. The wild chants coupled with physical exertion caused these priestesses to become "entheoi," i. e., "in the deity" or "filled with the spirit of that god." "At such times the ecstatic person had no consciousness of his own . . . the divinity spoke enclosed in the human body." Celsus is quoted as saying of these devotees that "both inside and outside the (heathen) sanctuaries people . . . uttered unknown, unintelligible speech."

Mohammedanism knows such phenomena, much like the pagan cases just mentioned. The Dervishes of Persia are wont to continue "uttering the name of Allah, accompanied by violent motions of the body till they work themselves into a frenzy, and fall into a trance foaming at the mouth." They are then accredited with miraculous gifts.

The "howling Dervishes," known as the Rufaiyah, place themselves in a certain "kneeling position while a swinging motion of the body is maintained." This position, or technique, is continued until the desired results appear, namely a fit of exhaustion or cataleptic stupor. Very much akin to this is the method of the "whirling Dervishes" who persist in a spinning movement until they reach "a state of religious exaltation which renders them partly unconscious, and during this ecstasy they preach moral sermons."

When Moses was empowered by God to show supernatural signs to Pharaoh "the magicians of Egypt did in like manner with their enchantments" in several instances. Moses' signs in Egypt were preparatory for the greater signs soon to appear at Sinai. But "Jannes and Jambres withstood Moses" as men always do who withstand the truth. Later, when the Babylonian sooth-sayer, Balaam, attempted to prophesy against Israel, God prevented him. But the fact of an intended curse turned into a blessing is no evidence that Balaam was "fully yielded" to God's Spirit. He "loved the hire of wrong-doing" and would gladly have earned the "hire" had he been able.

No more cases from paganism need now be cited. Enough has been said to show that "vision" and "ecstasy" and utterances of mysterious or meaningless words are found among heathen as well as among Christians. We dare not declare that all such phenomena are manifestations of the same spirit. But we may conclude that "prophesying" and "tongue talking" are not infallible proofs of the work of the Holy Spirit. The priests of paganism are able to produce the most deceptive counterfeit signs.

It is of utmost importance that on a subject of this kind we stand on the ground of Scripture. The Bible teaches us that there is a spiritual contact between God and man. Also that other spirits reach and influence mankind. The world lieth in the evil one. We are told not to believe every spirit, but to try them whether they are of God. A hankering for greatness and fame is easily mistaken for the voice of God. The Bible calls it "a vision of their own heart." (Jer. 23:16.) The prophecies from self-deceived prophets lead people astray: In times of moral darkness the strange actions and mysterious words of self-appointed prophets and prophetesses are most readily accepted. So it was in Israel of old, so it has ever been in the Church. "I sent not these prophets, yet they ran. I spake not unto them, yet they prophesied."

THE PLACE OF TONGUES IN SCRIPTURE

Tongues not included among spiritual fruits.

Tongues as listed in the New Testament

The purpose of the "accompanying signs" mentioned

in the Gospel by Mark.

O earth, earth, earth, hear the word of Jehovah (Jer. 22:29).

Thus saith Jehovah, Stand ye in the ways and see, and ask for the old paths, where is the good way; and walk therein, and ye shall find rest for your souls; but they said, We will not walk therein. And I set watchmen over you, saying, Hearken to the sound of the trumpet; but they said, We will not hearken (Jer. 6:16, 17).

Then certain of the scribes and Pharisees answered him, saying, Teacher, we would see a sign from thee. But he answered and said unto them, An evil and adulterous generation seeketh after a sign; and there shall no sign be given to it but the sign of Jonah the prophet (Matt. 12:38, 39).

Jesus saith unto him, Because thou hast seen me, thou hast believed: blessed are they that have not seen, but yet have believed (John 20:29).

But he said, Yea, rather blessed are they that hear the Word of God, and keep it (Luke 11:28).

Thy word have I laid up in my heart, That I might not sin against thee. Make me to understand the way of thy precepts: So shall I meditate on thy wondrous works. My soul melteth for heaviness: Strengthen thou me according unto thy word. Before I was afflicted I went astray; But now I observe thy word. The law of thy mouth is better unto me Than thousands of gold and silver. I beheld the treacherous, and was grieved, Because they observe not thy word (Psalm 119:11, 27, 28, 67, 72, 158).

I have given them thy word; and the world hated them, because they are not of the world. I pray not that thou shouldest take them from the world, but that thou shouldest keep them from the evil one. They are not of the world, even as I am not of the world (John 17:14, 16).

CHAPTER THREE

The Place of Tongues in Scripture

FROM the history of Christianity it should be plain to everyone that much—if not most—of the religious fervor within the Church which is expressed in the utterances commonly known as "speaking in tongues" have led men astray both in doctrine and in practice. Furthermore, that for ages such manifestations have been known in the heathen world. Still there are pious folk who sincerely believe that "tongues" is the surest token of a sanctified life, and therefore of greatest importance to Christian experience.

Now just what place do the Scriptures give to "speaking in tongues"? Do the New Testament writers emphasize the teaching of tongues as they do the fundamental doctrines of the Christian faith? Do the apostles teach that speaking in tongues is the most excellent gift, the most effective cause, or the choicest fruit of sanctification? If tongues are essential to the strong, Spirit-filled Christian life we should expect to find a clear statement to that effect. Indeed we might expect to find it repeated, stressed, and emphasized in several of the sacred writings.

What is written? How readest thou? Let us review a few of the most familiar Bible statements that have a direct bearing on spiritual life and living.

In speaking of faith and hope and love, the apostle tells us that these shall abide, but tongues shall cease (1 Cor. 13). In Col. 1:3-5, Paul gives thanks when he hears of the faith and love and hope of the Colossians. He does not rejoice over any tongue-talking in Colossae. Likewise in exhorting the Thessalonian disciples to steadfastness and spiritual sobriety, he mentions "putting on the breastplate of faith and love; and for a helmet, the hope of salvation" (1 Thess. 5:8). Evidently tongues was not an essential.

In the letters to the Romans and to the Ephesians much is said of growth in grace. "They that are after the Spirit, mind the things of the Spirit... the mind of the Spirit is life and peace" (Rom. 8:6-7). "Be ye therefore imitators of God as beloved children" (Eph. 5:1). Not a word about desiring any "baptism of tongues" in either of these two great doctrinal epistles. Nor do we find any hint that tongues make us rejoice in the Lord; not even in the beautiful joy-letter to the Philippians.

Few have ever measured up to Paul's passion for souls as it is expressed in Rom. 9:2-3. He had great sorrow and unceasing pain in his heart. He could wish to be accursed from Christ for his brethren's sake. In his ministry he was "in labors more abundantly, in prisons more abundantly, in stripes above measure, in deaths oft." Still no glory is given to tongues in this connection. And when he would stir us up to such zeal for the Lord that we too, present our bodies as a living sacrifice to Christ, he does not say that "tongues" would be of any help in our spiritual service.

The most inclusive Scripture passage in this connection is Gal. 5:22-23. "The fruit of the Spirit is love, joy, peace, longsuffering, kindness, goodness, faithfulness, meekness, self-control." This word describes the choicest of the Holy Spirit's work in sanctifying believers. It has always been, and will always be the highest aspirations and holiest standards of those who love Christ and are bearing *much* fruit for Him. It is the best evidence of the

Holy Spirit's power within. Yet not one word about the gift of "tongues"!

In the New Testament epistles wherein are delineated to us the chiefest teachings pertaining to a closer walk with God, do we find that Peter, Paul, James, or John, instruct the Elders or the teachers of the local churches to be instant in season and out of season exhorting men to speak in tongues? No such pastoral advice is ever given.

Speaking in tongues is not mentioned in three Gospels, nor in any of Paul's thirteen epistles except one, nor in the epistles of Peter, James, John, or Jude, nor in Hebrews, nor in Revelation.

Tongues is mentioned in Mark 16:17, as one of the signs that should follow the apostles. In Acts 2:4, 10:46, and 19:7, are three historic instances where tongues occurred. Finally, in 1 Cor. 12-14 we have references to the problem of tongues in Corinth. No more is found in the entire New Testament.

We shall briefly discuss the references given in Mark. And then give to Acts and the Corinthian case a somewhat fuller study.

In Mark 16:17-18 we read: "And these signs shall accompany them that believe: in my name shall they cast out demons; they shall speak with new tongues; they shall take up serpents, and if they drink any deadly thing, it shall in no wise hurt them; they shall lay hands on the sick and they shall recover."

Five *signs* are mentioned here. Notice that they are *signs,* not gifts. No one would speak of the "taking up of serpents" or of immunity to poison, as a "gift." Those signs should *accompany* the believers. They were to introduce the mystery of the Gospel to hostile Jew and sceptic Pagan. The "mystery" of the message was not due to the signs. Observe that the phrases: "God's wisdom in a mystery," "the mystery of Christ," "the mystery that hath been hid for ages and generations," "the mystery of the Kingdom," "the mystery of godliness," and many more, speak of that unsearchable mystery in God's plan of salvation, expressed in John 3:16.

That God would come in the flesh in order to save men who were His rebellious enemies is the mystery that even angels desire to look into. Such a plan of salvation is not the product of natural reasoning as we know reasoning. But nowhere are we told that we must have mystic signs or produce mysterious mutterings in order to accept the "mysterious gospel of free grace."

Just because such a gospel, such unheard-of "foolishness" was to be introduced, Christ gave to His ambassadors very special credentials. Dr. Remensnyder says in *The Post-Apostolic Age,* "This power He communicated to His apostles whom He sent forth. Without such a signal proof of divine sanction our Lord knew that it would be absolutely impossible to get the ears of men in introducing a religion so totally foreign to human ideas."

Men should be compelled, as it were, to take notice. The Gospel should have a hearing. But the credentials of the Church's divine authority are not to be taken as her mission, her spiritual purpose. After the Gospel had proved its power to regenerate man, then saved and sanctified men would be the Church's most convincing "sign."

The fruits of faith are a disciple's best credentials.

The disciples experienced the appearance of the signs mentioned in Mark 16:17. With the exception of the drinking deadly things, we know they were literally fulfilled in the Apostolic Church. (See Acts chapters 5, 10, 16, 28, etc.) Some of those signs are said to have appeared also in post-apostolic days in places where doors otherwise were closed to the Gospel.

But where the Word is being preached we know of no

conversions caused by signs of this kind. If men, who may hear the Gospel refuse to heed it, they will not believe though one rose from the dead.

Now, if among the aforementioned signs, the "new tongues" are pointed to as being the normal and universal evidence of the truest discipleship, why omit the rest? Why not seek the "baptism" of handling serpents, or drinking poison? Our Lord placed all these signs in the same class. When were pentecostals told to specialize in "tongues"?

To be sure, the casting out of demons and the healing of the sick are included by the tongues folk when and where that seems expedient, but the fact is that tongues is their *favorite* sign. Fanaticism and failure and fraud are not so easily detected in tongues as might be the case in attempting to exhibit the more miraculous tokens.

THE SIGNS OF TONGUES IN ACTS

The Old and the New Covenants compared.

A new era introduced.

The "tongues" of Pentecost.

The baptism of Cornelius.

The baptism of the twelve Ephesians.

Not a higher spiritual plane.

The truths established by the signs of tongues in Acts.

*The Gentiles are fellow-heirs, and fellow-members of
the body, and fellow-partakers of the promise in Christ
Jesus through the gospel ... to make all men see what
is the dispensation of the mystery which for ages hath
been hid in God who created all things; to the intent that
now unto the principalities and the powers in the heavenly
places might be made known through the church the
manifold wisdom of God* (Eph. 3:6, 9, 10).

*But now hath he obtained a ministry the more excel-
lent, by so much as he is also the mediator of a better
covenant, which hath been enacted upon better promises.
For if the first covenant had been faultless, then would no
place have been sought for a second. For this is the
covenant that I will make with the house of Israel after
those days, saith the Lord; I will put my laws into their
mind, and on their heart also will I write them: and I
will be to them a God, And they shall be to me a people*
(Hebrews 8:6, 7, 10).

*Having therefore, brethren, boldness to enter into the
holy place by the blood of Jesus, by the way which he
dedicated for us, a new and living way, through the veil,
that is to say, his flesh; and having a great priest over
the house of God; let us draw near with a true heart in
fulness of faith, having our hearts sprinkled from an evil
conscience; and having our body washed with pure
water, let us hold fast the confession of our hope that it
waver not; for he is faithful that promised* (Hebrews
10:19-23).

CHAPTER FOUR

The Signs of Tongues in Acts

THE signs of tongues as described in the book of Acts are the outstanding historic facts in this study. It is of the utmost importance to see the Lord's purpose in those manifestations.

Of course all will agree that the "speaking in tongues" on the Day of Pentecost, in Cornelius' home, and at the baptism of the Twelve Ephesians indicated the Holy Spirit's presence. And few, whether a pentecostal or not, will conclude that the Spirit's presence or power was *limited* to those three events. Scripture proofs to the contrary are too numerous.

Therefore it should not be difficult to agree that when God used special signs, He surely did so for a special purpose. We must not take that to be commonplace which He has made extraordinary. From all of Scripture we learn that God used supernatural means only when needed to establish supernatural facts. Such is God's economy in the Old and in the New Testaments.

In the next place, Bible readers must distinguish between the dispensation of the Old Testament and of the New Testament. If men jump back and forth from Moses to Paul, or from the prophets to the apostles in order to prove a dogma, without taking into account the difference between the Testaments, they are liable to arrive at strange conclusions.

There are no contradictions in Scripture, but the setting and scope, the predictions and fulfillments, the means and the message of the Old Covenant differ from those of the New.

When God ushers in a new era in His dealing with man, He ordinarily inaugurates that dispensation with special and supernatural signs and manifestations. So at the time of Noah (Gen. 9:12-13), at the time of Abraham (Gen. 15:17-18), and at the time of Moses (Exod. 19:16).

Taking the last-mentioned as an example, it would be absurd for pious Israelites to look for, or insist on seeing a smoking mountain, or hearing the awe-inspiring trumpet blast as the *normal experience of the chosen people* to be repeated at intervals, after that day. Not even the sprinkling of blood upon the book and upon the people was ever repeated (Exod. 24:7-8).

It is just as absurd and far more erroneous to believe that the "wonders in the heaven above and signs on the earth beneath" that ushered in the dispensation of the Holy Spirit shall be repeated in the Church. We are not to make that common and normal which the Lord has plainly indicated as special and super-normal.

The Old Covenant ended and the New took effect on the Day of Pentecost. That is established in Acts and the Epistles beyond question. We cannot overlook this if we would arrive at the fundamental difference between the "shadow" and the "substance" (Heb. 7:11—10:18). Christ Himself points to this vast difference when He says of even John the Baptist, the one nearest to New Covenant grace and truth: "He that is but little in the kingdom of heaven is greater than he."

With this in mind, we return to the record in the book of Acts. The three cases in Acts, where "tongues" are mentioned are Acts 2:4, 10:46, and 19:5-6. They are not the record of three Pentecosts. The second and third

We believe the answer that agrees with the Scriptures and is established by the history of the Church, is that *God ushered in a new era.* As stated already, when God does that, He reveals it by some extraordinary token. The manner in which it appeared was in accord with the prophecy of Joel in which he foretells of how the Spirit would be poured out on all flesh.

Pentecost must not be viewed from the spiritual standpoint alone, but also from the historical point of view. It was the beginning of a new dispensation of God among men.

It is a fact that generally speaking Christians of today are not Pentecost-conscious. We all have seen paintings and pictorial representations of the Child in the Bethlehem manger. Also we know many portrayals of the Risen Christ. On altars and in art-glass in churches and chapels all over Christendom there are countless representations of the Nativity and of the Resurrection. But few indeed are the paintings of the event that took place on the first Christian Pentecost. Granted that it may be difficult to represent on canvas the coming of the Spirit; we doubt that that is the only reason for the artists' omission. The truth is that we think less of Pentecost than we do of Christmas and Easter.

Christmas means much to us and yields much because we prepare much and expect much. For weeks and months we look forward to it. This is true, not only from the commercial and social points of view, but also from the religious, the spiritual viewpoint. Much effort is spent in Church and in Sunday School in order that our minds and hearts may be properly attuned to the blessed Christmas Gospel. And Christians are blessed. They experience the truth of the word: Be it unto thee according to thy faith.

Much the same is true of our Easter joy. A season of

definite preparation and expectation precedes the Easter Sunday services. There is something more, something higher and holier than the mere joy of spring in nature, that causes us to rejoice. It is the spring of souls, because "Christ hath burst His prison," and we are victors in the victorious Christ. But would Easter mean as much to us if it were scarcely mentioned before that Sunday morning?

What about Pentecost? Ask the Sunday School pupils what this day means to them, or what took place that day nineteen hundred years ago, and what answer do you get? Ask the average church-goer what he expects from Pentecost, and he will not understand what you mean. He expects nothing, and gets nothing. Again it is unto us according to our faith—or our lack of faith. Perhaps we need to remind one another that had there been no Christian Pentecost, the angelic messages of Christmas and Easter would avail us little. We would never have heard a Gospel word. We may well purpose prayerfully to become more Pentecost-minded.

Now by such a mind we do not mean that we should or would look for supernatural pentecostal signs, nor that our preparation should take the form of ecstasy or visions, and least of all any unseemly behavior. The signs are not needed now, but the power of the Holy Spirit is our urgent need. The Gift we have as Christians; His message of "the wonderful works of God" we all too frequently silence.

Again let it be said that the signs perceptible to the senses were simply tokens of the fact that the Gift now was come. The Holy Spirit was the gift that day. *He filled them, and thus they received His power.* This was a new measure of power such as had not been theirs heretofore. So great indeed was the difference that by comparison, He is spoken of as if He were not come to believers previous to this. From this time on everyone born of the Spirit, though he be "but little in the Kingdom of God," is greater than the greatest in Israel "born of woman."

The Gift would be received by the many (Acts 2:38); the supernatural signs thereof were received by the few. He was sent on that Pentecost when the Old Covenant was abolished and the New established (Hebr. 8:7) and He has not been taken from the Church since that day. It was the outpouring of the Spirit of adoption "whereby the people of God also became the children of God." It was the infilling and baptism of the one Body of the glorified Christ.

Before that day believers are not spoken of as the "body of Christ." From that time forth Christ's Holy Spirit dwells in the Church to quicken, to direct, to use it. Previous to this, the Spirit of God is spoken of (with few exceptions) as being *over* and *among* His people; now the Third Person in the Godhead takes His permanent abode *in* the believers (Acts 2:38; 5:32; Rom. 8:9-11; I Cor. 6:19; Gal. 4:6; II Cor. 1:21-22, etc.).

That day was not simply "the first Christian Pentecost" with others like it to follow. It is the *one* birthday of the Church. Never do the apostles speak of any other "Pentecost" in the churches where they worked.

How should they recognize the Spirit's advent? The outpouring must needs be an *objective fact* as well as a *subjective* experience, for it concerned the future, not of a few disciples, but of the entire Church. How might Peter and his fellow-disciples know with absolute certainty and assurance just *when* their waiting was ended and their commission to go into effect?

Were they to expect some particular "feeling" in the matter? Jesus had not promised that, nor is there the slightest Scriptural evidence that the twelve or the others

had any vision, or even ecstatic feelings. The apostles
were as different temperamentally and otherwise as any
twelve disciples very well can be. If the proof of the Holy
Spirit's presence should be subjective only, then surely
there might be more or less uncertainty and doubt.

Would God leave such an issue to be guessed at? Was
not the way of salvation in Christ about to be offered to
mankind? *Surely, God in His omnipotence and wisdom
would not leave His disciples in the slightest doubt or uncertainty in such an hour.* No, they were not left in uncertainty. The Lord "being therefore by the right hand
of God exalted and having received of the Father the
promise of the Holy Spirit" did pour forth that which
was seen and heard that day.

We find not the slightest hesitation now in the minds
of the apostles. They knew what the tokens indicated.
Therefore Peter with "the eleven" immediately refuted
the scoffers, and boldly asserted *"This is that"* which had
been predicted by Joel and by John and now graciously
fulfilled by Jesus Christ.

The extraordinary signs on the day of Pentecost were
given to remove every doubt, to assure every hope of His
flock, and *to signify to all Jerusalem that the crucified
Jesus was indeed the victorious Christ in whose Name
alone there now would be salvation.*

The next instance of tongues is that at the conversion
of Cornelius and his household. This is recorded fully
in the tenth and eleventh chapters of Acts.

The story is familiar to every Bible reader. One thing
we want to keep in mind pertaining to Cornelius, namely,
that he is the *first Gentile* (Acts 11:18) accepted into the
Christian Church. He was a sincere seeker for peace with
God. Such seeking and prayer God will graciously answer by sending the truth and light of His Gospel. No
doubt Cornelius had some knowledge of the God of Israel

to whom he prayed, but he was not a proselyte such as the Ethiopian eunuch apparently was. Cornelius was simply a devout Gentile, as yet outside of both Judaism and Christianity.

Cornelius sought God and found Him—not in nature, nor in philosophy, nor in philanthropy, nor even in his prayers. He found God when he heard and believed the Gospel of a crucified and risen Christ, the Lord who is rich unto all that call upon Him.

Then we may ask: Why was there *a special token* of the Holy Spirit's work in Cornelius, when we know of none such at the baptism of the Ethiopian or the converts in Lydda and Joppa? Surely, the Lord must have had a special reason for it. *Something new and unexpected was taking place.*

Bible readers are familiar with the deep-seated antipathy in the mind and heart of every Jew toward anything pertaining to a Gentile. It was utterly unthinkable to a faithful Jew that God would save a Gentile without first making him a proselyte by circumcision and other ordinances. Any Jew who taught otherwise was "not fit to live" (Acts 22:22).

Thus it was that for several years the apostles were unable to realize the inclusiveness of the Christian Church. Hence a special lesson was given to Peter in Joppa in order to compel him to minister to a Gentile in Caesarea.

We notice his hesitation and concern as he entered Cornelius' home. That his fears and forebodings were well-founded is plain from what followed later in Jerusalem.

In this instance, the manifestation of the Holy Spirit appeared *before* these Gentiles had been baptized. Had not this occurred, Peter would not at that time have dared to baptize them, even though he had ventured to preach to them. This is evident from Peter's first words after having seen the divine token. He stopped preaching. Turning to the Christians, "those of the circumcision," present, he said: "Can any man *forbid* the water that these should not be baptized?"

We note that the manifestation itself was Peter's chief defense later when he had to answer for such an unheard-of procedure to the brethren in Jerusalem (11:17). The apostle said: "The Holy Spirit fell on them, even as on us at the beginning." That argument was effective. They who formerly had contended with him now realized that God had broken down that "middle wall of partition" between Jew and Gentile. So they held their peace and glorified God.

The token of the Spirit's presence in the house of Cornelius cannot by any Biblical interpretation be called a "second blessing"; yet the sign was identical to that in Jerusalem, and later in Ephesus. Nor was it granted in answer to any "prayer, looking forward to a baptism in the Holy Spirit." As we have pointed out, even the believers were amazed at this event.

Let us not overlook the significant fact that when Peter vindicates himself before the Jewish brethren, he refers directly back to what had occurred years before on the Day of Pentecost. "The Holy Spirit fell on them even as on us *at the beginning.*" The inference is plain that in all the intervening years there had been no such manifestations to which Peter could appeal. The sign of tongues was a sign of "the beginning"; also in this phase of the "beginning." Incidentally this word of Peter indicates quite the opposite of what some modern pentecostals would have us believe, namely that all believers in the apostolic days had the power to speak in tongues.

We have seen also that this very sign was repeated just before the baptism of the *first* Gentile. The Lord thereby stopped the mouth of the Jewish Christians. The conclusion in this case is obvious: The purpose of the extraordinary manifestation was to assure the messengers and to convince the doubters of God's new order in the Kingdom. They were thereby made to see that "here is neither Jew nor Greek ... for ye are all *one* in Christ Jesus." Now the Church had begun among the Gentiles.

The last instance of speaking in tongues told of in Acts, is found in 19:1-7. This narrative has occasioned many and strange interpretations. Some seem to think that every "believer" is a Christian, regardless of what he believes. Others fail utterly to distinguish between the preparatory baptism administered by John the Baptist, and the Christian baptism instituted by Christ on the day of Ascension.

In verses 5 to 7 we read: "And when they heard this, they were baptized into the name of the Lord Jesus. And when Paul had laid his hands upon them, the Holy Spirit came on them; and they spake with tongues, and prophesied. And they were in all about twelve men."

Once more we are confronted with the question *why* God made this event in Ephesus an occasion for special or extraordinary tokens of the Holy Spirit's work.

We have seen that in the two previous instances there were certain doubts and prejudices to be removed and certain facts and doctrines to be established. Furthermore, we know that these doctrines were fundamental in the missionary program of the Church for all succeeding generations.

We may now ask: what fundamental truth, if any, would the Lord teach the Church by that which took place under Paul's ministry on that day in Ephesus?

Let us glance at the situation. Paul had not worked long in Ephesus when he met a group of "disciples." Most probably they were Alexandrian Jews such as Apollos. They were disciples of John the Baptist and "were looking for the early advent of the Messiah in the flesh, and had prepared for His coming by receiving the baptism of John. ... They had confessed their sins and had been baptized with the baptism of repentance, but they did not know of faith in Jesus as the Messiah they were expecting," nor did they know of "regeneration by that faith, its seal of baptism in His Name, or the gift of the Holy Spirit."

It is evident that those twelve "disciples" in Ephesus were exactly in the same religious position as were any penitent Jew, who in the years past had been baptized by John in the Jordan. That is, *spiritually they were still on Old Testament ground.*

Of course Paul soon realized the situation, and therefore asked a question that would immediately show to these men the vital difference between the baptism which *they* had received, and the baptism of Christians. It indicated and implied the difference between the Old Covenant of the Law and the New Covenant of Grace. The Holy Spirit's abiding presence from the day of Pentecost made this difference. But of His ministry the twelve in Ephesus knew nothing.

Paul at once proceeded to instruct the twelve men regarding faith in Jesus *for that was the point in which their "belief" had been amiss.* Then he baptized them into the Name of the Lord just as he and thousands of others had been baptized.

As the final act at the baptism, Paul laid his hands upon them. That was a customary form of benediction at baptism in the early Church. It had been done also to Paul when he was baptized. "And when Paul had laid his hands upon them, the Holy Spirit came on them, and they spake with tongues and prophesied."

Again the sign of tongues. Why? These men were not heathen; they were of the Jewish people. They were not the first Jews of the dispersion to be baptized. Hundreds had been received into the Church in Antioch and elsewhere before the baptism of these twelve "disciples" in Ephesus. There was no "beginning" to establish in this case.

Then, too, we see that the token of the Holy Spirit's presence appeared *after* the baptism in this case. What would the Lord teach us here?

We do not read of any gift of tongues when Jews were baptized in Lydda or in Joppa. Neither at the baptism of Lydia, or even of the jailor in Philippi. Evidently there was no need of any external sign at those baptisms for they were ordinary instances of Jews and of Gentiles being received by baptism into the Christian Church.

But the twelve "disciples" in Ephesus did need a special New Testament truth impressed upon them. They were only disciples of John, though they and others may have imagined that thereby they were Christians. They had been baptized years before Paul arrived, but *not with the Christian baptism.*

The "disciples" in Ephesus, therefore, needed some special token from God to make it clear to them—and to all disciples ever after—that the baptism they *now* had received at the hand of Paul was not just another baptism, more or less like any other and of little consequence. They were to learn that there was a vast difference; in fact so great a difference that Paul dealt with them exactly as if they never had been baptized. Paul set aside the baptism of John altogether.

The gift of the Holy Spirit was theirs when they believed Paul's message about Christ and were baptized into Him. If the sign of tongues had appeared *before* the baptism in this case it would have indicated that their first baptism was a "Christian" baptism minus the gift of the Holy Spirit. But now the sign of God's approval appeared after the new, the Christian, baptism had been administered.

Thereby three important doctrines were established. These Ephesians were made to see that *now they received the Holy Spirit,* which they had not in their former discipleship. Further this clarified to them that they were now in *a new position* in the Kingdom of God. Finally it was an object lesson to them what the apostle later writes of to the believers in this same city of Ephesus, namely that *in the Church there is "one baptism."*

One more observation may be useful, relative to the three instances in Acts which we have discussed: Did the baptisms "with signs" bestow permanent blessings, *different* from the grace and power bestowed to others, of whom nothing is said pertaining to tongues or visible manifestations?

We want to learn from evidence out of the Scriptures whether or not the converts in Caesarea and Ephesus were on a higher plane spiritually than their fellow Christians elsewhere.

Peter had labored in Joppa as well as in nearby Caesarea. Paul had baptized believers in Philippi before he ministered to those in Ephesus. Aside from their first testimonies and "prophecies," are there any Biblical proofs that the household of Cornelius or the twelve Ephesians were more powerful or useful in the Church of Christ than was Dorcas or Lydia? Surely every candid Christian will agree that there is no such evidence in the Bible.

And what about the assertion so frequently made in certain groups that "Spirit baptism with tongues" is given in answer to prayer for such gifts? Likewise that every believer may and ought to experience such a "baptism" and will experience it if he only is persistent in praying for it? What saith the Scriptures?

The Scriptures do not say that the first disciples had a "ten-day prayer meeting in order to get the gift of the

Holy Spirit"! Those who intentionally make such statements wrest the Word of God to suit their own notions. Nor does the Bible tell us that the supernatural manifestations on the day of Pentecost came in answer to the continued and steadfast prayers of the disciples.

The question whether or not there were previous prayers for a "spirit baptism with tongues" is more easily determined in the other two cases in the book of Acts. It will bear repetition to emphasize that neither Peter in Caesarea nor Paul in Ephesus is spoken of as having prayed perseveringly for a "spirit baptism with tongues" upon the people to whom they ministered. As for the persons who were baptized, it is absurd to maintain that *they* had sought in advance for any particular evidence of the Holy Spirit's presence or power. In neither case had they knowledge of the Person of the Holy Spirit, much less of His work in the hearts of men.

Let us bear in mind as we restate the purposes of the manifestations, that we speak not of the Spirit's coming and abiding but of special tokens thereof. They indicate the completion in the founding of the Church to the end that (1) all men in Jerusalem should know that the promise was fulfilled and the Holy Spirit was come to abide in the Church; a new dispensation was begun among men. (2) In the Christian Church the wall of partition between Jew and Gentile is forever taken away. They are one in Christ Jesus. (3) No other baptism but the one instituted and commanded by Christ when He gave His commission shall be accepted as a baptism of Christians.

Who shall say that these truths were not of such vital and far-reaching importance to Christianity as to warrant special revelations and assurances!

THE CORINTHIAN TONGUES

A problem in the congregation.
Religious inflation in Corinth.
The grace-gifts classified.
The connection between the three chapters.
Corinthian tongues described.
Apostolic exhortations and injunctions.
What were the Corinthian reactions?

And I, brethren, could not speak unto you as unto spiritual, but as unto carnal, as unto babes in Christ. I fed you with milk, not with meat; for ye were not yet able to bear it: nay, not even now are ye able; for ye are yet carnal: for whereas there is among you jealousy and strife, are ye not carnal, and do ye not walk after the manner of men? (I Cor. 3:1-3).

For who maketh thee to differ? and what hast thou that thou didst not receive? but if thou didst receive it, why dost thou glory as if thou hadst not received it? Already are ye filled, already ye are become rich, ye have come to reign without us (I Cor. 4:7-8a).

But all these worketh the one and the same Spirit, dividing to each one severally even as he will. For as the body is one, and hath many members, and all the members of the body, being many, are one body; so also is Christ. For in one Spirit were we all baptized into one body, whether Jews or Greeks, whether bond or free; and were all made to drink of one Spirit. For the body is not one member, but many (I Cor. 12:11-14).

For God is not a God of confusion, but of peace. As in all the churches of the saints. If any man thinketh himself to be a prophet, or spiritual, let him take knowledge of the things which I write unto you, that they are the commandment of the Lord. But if any man is ignorant, let him be ignorant (I Cor. 14:33, 37, 38).

But I fear, lest by any means, as the serpent beguiled Eve in his craftiness, your minds should be corrupted from the simplicity and the purity that is toward Christ (II Cor. 11:3).

CHAPTER FIVE

The Corinthian Tongues

A S far as we can ascertain, the "tongues" in Acts of which we have spoken did not cause any problem within the congregations or groups where they occurred. Apparently the tongues mentioned in Acts were recognized for what they were, namely, extraordinary signs for extraordinary purposes.

But the Corinthian tongues was a serious congregational problem. That is very evident from what Paul has to say about the matter. The greater part of three chapters of the first Epistle to the Corinthians is devoted to this discussion. Therefore those chapters call for careful study.

We shall not attempt a detailed exegetical study in this treatise. But we shall observe first the spiritual tone of the Corinthian Church as depicted throughout the entire epistle. Next we would indicate the position of the said three chapters in the relation to preceding chapters, and to each other. And finally note Paul's method and message in dealing with the problem.

Perhaps it is of more than passing interest to us to recall what kind of a city Corinth was at the time of Paul. It was a cosmopolitan city on account of its commerce with both East and West. Merchants and sailors and adventurers flocked to Corinth. To be "a Corinthian" was to be a profligate. The city was also a center of Greek religious influence. The notorious shrine of Aphrodite was situated on Mt. Corinthus at the southern border of the city. A thousand priestesses conducted their licentious rites in that temple.

The Corinthian Church had many gifted members. "Ye come behind in no gift" (I Cor. 1:7). In that respect they probably measured up to any of the apostolic churches. By gifts the apostle means something more than natural talent or endowment though they are not necessarily excluded. There were "wisdom," "knowledge," "faith," "healings," etc. (I Cor. 12:8-10), both natural and supernatural abilities spoken of as gifts and as signs given by God's Spirit and intended for the Church's benefit.

However, a gifted church is not necessarily a spiritually strong church; nor an edifying and useful church. In spite of its many able members, it may be a carnal, selfish, and altogether unlovely congregation; a veritable caricature of what the New Testament saints should be.

Such was the Corinthian Church. Spiritually it was on a low plane. Its worldly traits were so predominant that we need only mention them, to see the utterly "carnal" state of this congregation.

Spiritual vanity and pride were the besetting sins of the Corinthian Christians. Self-esteem of that sort expresses itself in various ways. The Corinthians were developing a distaste for the preaching of the plain Word of God, they favored something more "mysterious" with a sprinkling of Greek "wisdom." Therefore they catered to eloquent men. They even misconstrued Paul's willingness to forego material support from them. Despising the unadorned message and humble messenger, we also find them despising the Lord's Table, and questioning the doctrine of resurrection.

Of course such attitude to the revealed Word bare its legitimate fruit in life and conduct. Factions, dishonesty, and lawsuits were common. Adultery, fornication, was more than condoned; it was boasted as evidence of liberty. One might expect that the institution of marriage also would be in low esteem, and that "personal liberty" would ride rough-shod over the scruples of weaker brethren. Furthermore we have here the first instances of women taking such liberties in the life and rule of the congregation that they caused offense both within and without the church.

What was the underlying cause of Corinthianism? *Spiritual pride!* Again and again the apostle uses the phrase "puffed up"! *It was a pronounced case of religious inflation!*

Notice the warnings against self-seeking (10:24, 13:5, 14:12), likewise contentiousness (5:9, 11:16, 16:14). Note how all of chapter thirteen exhorts to kind consideration of others. Indeed the words: "Let all that ye do be done in love" (16:14) may well be taken as the key-verse to the entire epistle. If anyone will read 4:6-10, 4:18, 5:2, 14:37, and practically all of chapters 8 and 12, he will see how haughty, "filled," "strong," "glorious," and self-sufficient was the church in Corinth.

The marvel is that the apostle will at all recognize those people as disciples! He certainly exposes and denounces that brand of discipleship. They were "carnal" when he worked among them; they were "yet carnal" when he later addressed them by letter.

Why emphasize these facts about the Corinthians? Because above all others, those people gloried in much speaking in tongues.

After Paul has dealt with several problems, one after another, he says in 12:1: "Now concerning spiritual gifts, brethren, I would not have you ignorant." Then follows the discussion in chapters 12, 13, 14. These three chapters deal with *one* problem and must be studied as a unit if one would learn the lesson of each chapter.

It may aid us in following this discussion to keep in mind the writer's arrangement. First, he points out the *unity of source* of these gifts. They are all bestowed by the one Holy Spirit (ch. 12). Next he emphasizes the motive or *attitude* in which all gifts must function, namely in love which is greater than any other attainment (ch. 13). And lastly, he states the *purpose* of all grace-gifts, which is to edify the church. He also shows the relative value of each, particularly with reference to tongues (ch. 14).

In detail the apostle compares the several gifts to members of the human body. It were absurd for one limb to despise another, though their appearance and function were different. So it were inexcusable and wicked for one Christian to belittle or to envy the grace-gift of another. The one Spirit imparted and varied the gifts as it pleased Him.

No one could claim any special "baptism" or higher degree of spirituality as the source of his particular gift. "In one Spirit were we all baptized into *one* body ... and were all made to drink of *one* Spirit" (12:13). As everywhere else, so also here does Paul recognize only one baptism. The baptism had been alike for *all,* yet not all were prophets, nor teachers, nor spoke with tongues.

Paul enumerates the grace-gifts. Some of them are listed three times in chapter twelve. In each tabulation is also a classification. This is not at all as the Corinthians evidently had evaluated them. Tongues and related gifts, so far from being signs of superior piety, are placed at the very bottom of the list.

Let Christians earnestly and humbly desire the enduements that are truly the greater! Put first things first!

But the apostle does not therewith end his statement. Whether gifts be great or small, a carnal grading would be degrading them. He would show them a far better, "a most excellent way" in the use of spiritual accomplishments (ch. 12).

Suppose that one did speak with tongues, even angelic tongues, what then? Suppose he also possessed all the other supernatural gifts, what profit were it if he were proud and puffed up over it? Or how could the grace-gifts edify the other Christians if accompanied by self-seeking, and not motivated by love? All mysterious words were only so much sound, and all miraculous deeds were worthless unless inspired by Christian love (ch. 13).

Furthermore any gift missed its mark if it did not serve to edify the Church. It were a failure if used to attract attention to man. Such was the case with tongues as depicted in chapter fourteen. "No man understandeth," "he edifieth himself," "the other is not edified." We can sense a divine irony in Paul's word to some of the misled zealots: "So also ye, *since ye are zealous* of spiritual gifts, seek that ye may abound unto the edifying of the church."

Consequently the ability to speak in tongues was in no wise a mark of the deepest spiritual experience. Other gifts were far more useful and more to be desired. Indeed tongues were even worse than useless whenever manifested in public without being interpreted or without control (ch. 14).

Just what were the Corinthian "tongues," and what does the apostle teach us with reference to the use and misuse of this gift?

Bible scholars who have made the most thorough study of this subject are agreed that the gift of tongues in Corinth was related to the sign in Jerusalem, Caesarea, and Ephesus, *but of a decidedly inferior type*. We would add that this was probably one of the many instances where men have caused a blessing to become a bane or even worse by using it for their own aggrandizement. Thereby they made them not only a "lower grade of tongues," but opened the way for blending them with actual counterfeits.

The tongues spoken of in Acts were intelligible to the human mind. No interpreter was needed.

Not so in Corinth. The utterances were evidently not

in any foreign language. "No man understandeth." "There is no evidence that the miracle of tongues consisted in the speaking of one of the known languages not previously acquired" (Kuyper). The words were not translated as if from one language to another, but "interpreted," that is, explained, made intelligible. Hence the special gift of interpretation was necessary if tongues should be used. The speaking was directed to God. The utterances were controlled by the emotions, the spirit; not by the mind, or intellect.

From these descriptive phrases found in chapter fourteen we conclude that *the best of Corinthian "tongues" was a mystic communing with God, an ecstatic form of private prayer and praise.* In public such utterances, without being interpreted, would be "speaking into the air" (14:9).

If the gift of tongues in Corinth ever had been of the perfect type of Pentecost, it apparently had degenerated before the time Paul wrote of it as a problem.

In the first place, note that it was a problem of deep concern to the more sober-minded members of the church. We have pointed out previously that there seems to have been something questionable in the manifestation of the supernatural gifts among the Corinthians. Apparently it reminded them of their past heathen worship. Paul had to reassure the brethren that no messenger filled with God's Spirit would curse the Name of Jesus (I Cor. 12:2-3).

It is altogether probable that pagan priests in their weird frenzies had been heard to speak just such blasphemies. Something similar occurred later in Ephesus (Acts 19:15). May it have been that the actions and utterances of the tongue-talkers even within the church were shockingly similar to the ways of the heathen?

Speaking of the evident degeneration of tongues in Corinth, one must not overlook a significant phrase in chapter thirteen. It mentions *unseemly* behavior (13:5). Keep in mind that in this chapter "love" is contrasted with certain gifts, tongues in particular. In making the comparison the apostle says: "Love doth not behave itself unseemly"! Is it a far-fetched inference to say that perhaps Paul had heard of *unseemly behavior* on the part of tongue-talkers?

Further on the evaluation of tongues as well as the attitude of those who exhibited that gift is said to be childish. Mature men were expected to use their minds as well as their emotions when partaking in public worship. "Brethren be not children in mind. . . . in mind be men."

All this, the similarity to pagan rites, the unseemly behavior, the childish attitude, is climaxed by the descriptive word "mad" (14:23). The form of the verb used signifies a drunken spree, or prophetic frenzy, or disorderly ecstasy. No wonder the "tongues movement" was a serious problem in Corinth! Instead of edifying the church, the net results were confusion. It is painfully evident that they were in need of instruction in this matter. "Concerning spiritual gifts, brethren, I would not have you ignorant."

Before leaving the study of the situation in Corinth, we would observe the Apostle's conclusions and commands regarding the use and misuse of the grace-gifts.

"I would have you all speak with tongues" (14:5). That is, worship God also by this gift if you have it, but remember it is not the most blessed way; "I would *rather* that ye should prophesy." That may not give you such a thrill nor attract such attention, but it edifies your brethren. Furthermore, remember that if you *must* speak in tongues, *let it be in private,* in your own secret prayer closet! But not in the assembly, except it be interpreted.

"I speak in tongues more than you all." Hence you have no reason to assume superiority on that score. And still I do not exhibit and parade that power. Far from it.

Though I thank God for every form of exalted communion with Him in my private prayers, "yet in the church I had rather speak five words with my understanding, that I might instruct others also, than ten thousand words in a tongue."

"What is it then, brethren?" What is the conclusion of the whole matter? First and foremost, that all things be done unto edifying. Second, "tongues" shall be kept strictly under control: "two, or at the most three, and that in turn." Third, if there be no interpreter, the speaking in tongues is not permitted.

So far, these apostolic injunctions. Does modern pentecostalism observe and obey this Word? If not, we stand on Scriptural ground and say that their tongue-talking is sin.

How did the Corinthians receive this command pertaining to tongues? We do not know. Nothing is said about this in Paul's second letter to them.

But at the close of his discussion in the present chapter (I Cor. 14:34-40), three things arrest our attention. The one, namely, that Paul seems to have anticipated that the women would not take kindly to what had been said. Without a doubt, some Corinthian women were involved in the tongue-talking. Otherwise the apostle would have had no occasion to mention them in this connection. He tells them very plainly that the Word of God did not come from them (14:36). He did not accredit their revelation, if they claimed any such.

Then, too, a special reminder is directed to any individual who "thinketh himself to be a prophet or spiritual." Such a one must take notice of the apostolic word as *final* in any matter, for it is "the commandment of the Lord" (14:37).

And at the very conclusion Paul says: "Forbid not to speak with tongues." Here is divine wisdom! If there ever were inspired psychology, we have it here. "Forbid not"; thereby you give tongues occasion to be much in demand. Rather encourage public testimony in "prophecy"; let the better, more useful gift come to the fore. Thus by wise substitution the problem of tongues would be solved, and all things be done decently and in order.

Our natural bent is ever to differ with God in the evaluation of spiritual things. We regard the vessel more than the treasure. In this, as in all else, His thoughts are higher than our thoughts. So far from being evidence of true sanctification that men are attracted to the outward appearance of grace-gifts, it rather indicates that "man looketh on the outward appearance, but Jehovah looketh on the heart."

Search *me*, O God, and know *my* heart: try me, and know my thoughts; and see if there be any wicked way in me, and lead me in the way everlasting.

THE MODERN TONGUES MOVEMENT

The Irvingites.

The Holiness Movements in our country.

Examples of modern tongues.

Examples of modern prophetism.

Going beyond what is written.

And thou, son of man, set thy face against the daughters of thy people, that prophesy out of their own heart; and prophesy thou against them, and say, Thus saith the Lord Jehovah: Because with lies ye have grieved the heart of the righteous, whom I have not made sad, and strengthened the hands of the wicked, that he should not return from his wicked way, and be saved alive (Ezekiel 13:17-18a, 22).

And he said unto him, I also am a prophet as thou art; and an angel spake unto me by the Word of Jehovah ... But he lied unto him (I Kings 13:18).

Take heed lest there shall be any one that maketh spoil of you through his philosophy and vain deceit, after the tradition of men, after the rudiments of the world, and not after Christ: for in him dwelleth all the fulness of the Godhead bodily, and in him ye are made full, who is the head of all principality and power (Col. 2:8-10).

These are springs without water, and mists driven by a storm; for whom the blackness of darkness hath been reserved. For uttering great swelling words of vanity, they entice in the lusts of the flesh, by lasciviousness, those who are just escaping from them that live in error; promising them liberty, while they themselves are bondservants of corruption; for of whom a man is overcome, of the same is he also brought into bondage (II Peter 2:17-19).

The lamp of thy body is thine eye: when thine eye is single, thy whole body also is full of light; but when it is evil, thy body also is full of darkness. Look therefore whether the light that is in thee be not darkness. If therefore thy whole body be full of light, having no part dark, it shall be wholly full of light, as when the lamp with its bright shining doth give thee light (Luke 11:34-36).

CHAPTER SIX

The Modern Tongues Movement

JUST how closely the modern tongues movement is related to Corinthianism and to the sporadic fanaticism of later eras anyone may learn simply by observing the dominant traits and teachings of pentecostal sects as we find them today.

We recall story after story of folks carried away by the pentecostal type of religious enthusiasm. In nearly every instance it is the same pitiful, sordid, satanic delusion. Even the grossest license becomes to them the expression of a most perfect liberty.

Perhaps the most familiar pentecostal group of the nineteenth century are the Irvingites. They are named for their leader, Edward Irving, born in 1792, who was a pastor in London.

Irving had heard of spiritual quickening in several sections of the British Isles. He longed for similar blessings for himself and his own flock. Being a man of tense emotional temperament, he was prone to value subjective experiences above all else as proofs of true faith. He and his followers persisted in prayer for miraculous tokens of the Spirit's presence in their midst. The burden of their prayers was for a renewal of the signs of Pentecost.

Presently Irving's congregation in London began to have strange experiences. One member after another became endued with a mysterious power by which they uttered unintelligible words. Occasionally they lapsed into a trance or into a cataleptic state. Then they frequently "prophecied" in their native language.

This spectacular type of revival swept many ardent Christians off their feet. They had long besought God for a revived church, and this seemed to be an answer to their prayers. True, a number of lukewarm or slothful believers were convicted of sin and truly quickened. But a great many more broke loose from their religious moorings and drifted into the grossest kinds of error.

The plain words of the Scriptures did not satisfy those who joined Irving. They persisted unceasingly for days and nights in calling for "the baptism of tongues." Of course, a "baptism" eventually came, as we have stated.

"Apostles" and "prophets" arose in their midst also, claiming to be the true successors of the Twelve. Their messages were said to be inspired, and even of higher authority than the Bible. Frequently the revelations of the Irvingite apostles came in direct conflict with the written Word. This is probably why they did not hesitate to denounce Bible societies as "the curse which walks through the land killing the spirit through the letter."

After some time they, who were of a more conservative disposition, realized that the Irvingite movement was a delusion. One who had been a noted convert, says in his *Narrative of Facts:* "It was manifest to me that the power was supernatural; it was therefore a spirit. It seemed to me to bear witness to the work and the fruits of the Spirit of God. The conclusion was inevitable that it was the Spirit of God, and if so the deduction was immediate that it ought in all things to be obeyed. . . . Awful, therefore, is the mistake if a seducing spirit is entertained as the Holy Spirit of Jehovah. The more devoted the Christian seduced, the more implicit the obedience to the seducing spirit" (Baxter in *Gift of Tongues* by Anderson).

The Irvingite cult is not much in evidence now, but its

spiritual descendants are with us. The story of the origin, acts, and fruitage of this movement teaches us the same solemn truth namely, that if men go beyond the Scriptures in their search for spiritual power, they will indeed be spirit-filled, but not by the Holy Spirit.

This truth is abundantly verified by the developments of American pentecostalism. Space does not permit, nor does the case require that we rehearse the countless stories of the tongues movement. A few references will suffice to show how closely American pentecostalism is related to the religious vagaries of the past.

Toward the close of the last century a revival in several denominations in England and America brought with it a by-product that has been known as "the Holiness Movement." Several groups left the church because it was "too dead."

As a result, a number of new "holy" sects sprang up, particularly in the Southern states of our country. These sects differed from one another in some respects, but all were alike in demanding a "full restoration of the gifts to the church," more especially the gift of tongues.

The following instances are typical of the beginnings and the developments in nearly every case:

In 1900 a small group in Topeka, Kansas, met to study the baptism in the Spirit. *They did not study much else in the Scriptures.* The "baptism with signs" was their one doctrine and desire. A woman in this group says: "During the first days of 1901 . . . I began to speak in tongues glorifying God. I talked several languages and it was clearly manifest when a new dialect was spoken." The headquarters of the group was a certain Bible school in Topeka. The head of the school and leader of the tongue talkers was a man of unsavory reputation. His morals and ethics were such that the civil authorities of more than one state had charges preferred against him.

Thereafter we find Los Angeles to be a new Corinth of tongues. The old leaders who had fallen into disrepute in Texas and Kansas had pitched their tents in Los Angeles. It must be said to the honor of the Los Angeles group that they very soon disowned the "apostles" from the East. But their works followed them, and continued.

In Los Angeles the special place of meeting was an old barn-like building on Azusa Street. It was known as the Azusa Street Mission. The folks there had heard of the tongues movement in Kansas. Insistently they too cried to God for a "second Pentecost."

Finally the signs appeared. Men and women were possessed by a strange power that made them fall down and pour forth torrents of sounds which no one could understand. To them it was the "latter rain" of a new pentecostal dispensation.

The Los Angeles movement spread far and wide, even to Europe, Australia and the Orient. Men who observed the manifestations were in doubt whether to scoff or to pray.

However, here, too, the enthusiasm soon went from confusion to mania. The lasting fruits were licentiousness, wrecked family life, and incurable insanity. One quotation will suffice: "Certain 'sisters' within the Tongues Movement in our city advised this lady (name omitted) that inasmuch as her husband was not sympathetic with the Tongues brand of religion, their marriage was not *'in the Lord.'* Therefore, they advised her that it would be perfectly proper for her to ignore this marriage and to enter into 'a spiritual alliance' with a certain Tongues preacher. This she did! She ... went away with this preacher to conduct Pentecostal meetings over the country. Another wrecked home! Another fine family bowing its head in disgrace and shame! Another bitter fruit of this demoniacal movement!"

Disgust and dismay will grip almost anyone who traces this movement in our land. Not that gross error is not found occasionally also in the most conservative churches. Especially does it appear in the wake of a strong and sound spiritual reviving. Some tares there will be growing among the wheat. Still we may count the erring ones as the exceptions. But in the Tongues Movement it seems as if fanaticism, and sensuality and insanity are not the exception, but the rule!

One writer describes his observations: "In company with a sober brother I went for the first time in San Francisco. The place was crowded. A large fleshy woman was leading the meeting amid great excitement. Strangely enough, we were hardly seated when she cried out, 'We need to pray; two enemies of the truth have just come in. The spirit tells me they are here to fight the truth. But I warn them they are fighting against God' . . . The meeting went on. . . Presently we were electrified by hearing for the first time the weird, piercing notes of a woman under the 'power,' speaking in 'tongues.' I took careful note of every syllable, and jotted them down: 'Ku-ri-ah, Ku-ri-ah, Ku-ri-ah, Ku-ri-ah-ke.' This she repeated over and over till almost out of breath, while the rest shouted with delight at this evidence of the spirit's control!"

"In Portland, Oregon, . . . what we saw and heard beggars description. The excitement was nerve-racking. As many as a dozen prayed—rather *screamed*—at one time. 'Tongues' were much in evidence, and here there were interpreters too. . . Almost at our feet a man fell over on his back, writhing and foaming as in an epileptic fit. I suggested getting him out of the close, hot room. . . 'Keep your hands off God's ark,' someone shouted. 'This is the Holy Ghost.' For forty minutes by the clock he writhed there on the floor and at last fell back limp and lay as though dead. Then a 'worker' jumped on his breast, put his mouth to the unconscious man's nose, and cried, 'Receive ye the Holy Ghost!' and blew powerfully into the nostrils. This was repeated over and over again—a most disgusting spectacle. Finally the man opened his eyes, rose, and sat quietly on a chair, weary, and with no apparent result. . . I was told afterwards of seven persons sent to insane asylums from that mission; and I saw and conversed with a baldheaded girl of about seventeen, who had contracted brainfever through the unnatural excitement, and had lost her hair in her illness." (Ironside.)

In Seattle the story is repeated. One writer tells of a recent case that ended in stark madness and double murder. "Mr. Blank and family came frequently to my church. He was considered to be a well-meaning, sincere Christian. Late one evening he came . . . to inform me that he had recently made some 'startling new discoveries in religious matters' . . . Since this 'discovery' was made he had been 'compelled by the Holy Spirit to be re-baptized in the Name of Jesus,' and that then he 'received the baptism of fire, and the power of the Holy Ghost'. . . Efforts to reason with him on the basis of Holy Scripture seemed futile."

This man eventually had a quarrel with the pentecostal leader who had baptized him. "On a Saturday morning the pentecostal leader went to the home of Mr. Blank. Mr. Blank in a violent rage met him at the door and refused him admittance. . . Later (speaking to the police), the leader said, 'He is not insane, but he is troubled with a demoniac spirit, and tomorrow morning my congregation will pray it out of him'."

Soon the tragedy was discovered. In a bedroom were found the bodies of his two boys, nine and eleven years old,—"a sacrifice to religious fanaticism." The man, of course, claimed to have been led by the spirit to murder his children.

This same author also quotes other cases from Washington, West Virginia, Ohio, Arkansas, etc., etc., all ending in shattered faith, mind, or home.

The Middle West section of the country affords no exception to this rule. Late one summer evening two young men walked down a Minneapolis street and noticed a group of excited people standing at the entrance of an assembly hall. The two men heard a commotion from upstairs and went up to investigate.

In the rear of a hall they found a dozen men and women crowding about a young woman who was lying on the floor, semi-conscious, and in a most indecent position. Her brother was trying to get her out and away, but the others prevented him. No one was permitted to arouse her. "The spirit is doing this work," it was claimed.

The two young men and the girl's brother finally went out and told a policeman. "Are they at it again?" he exclaimed. "I'll clear them out." In a few moments this "after-meeting" broke up, and the young girl was taken to her home.

Not long ago we happened into a large meeting conducted by a certain pentecostal group. A man preached; his sermon was for the most part Scriptural and was not sensational.

Just as he was about to close his address, a woman began to talk some gibberish. As near as we could distinguish, it was "massach, massach, massach." Her tongue talk seemed to electrify the audience. All over the assembly, men and women began to twitch and groan and mutter.

Then came a veritable exodus to the "prayer room" at the rear of the hall. In that place some thirty or more men and women hurried to get the "tongue baptism." Some knelt, others lay prostrate on the floor. All joined in a moaning, wailing chorus that was heard far outside the place of meeting. The hideous screaming began about nine o'clock. It continued till after midnight.

In a previous chapter we made mention of a religious phenomenon appearing in our own day which has many things in common with the tongues movement. That is the prophetism of West Africa. One may say that it more closely resembles the Montanism of the Early Church than any thing that has appeared since the time of Montanus. A brief glimpse of what this twentieth century prophet movement is like may be instructive in more ways than one.

W. J. Platt, an English Missionary to West Africa for nearly twenty years, tells us in his recent book, *From Fetish to Faith* (London 1935) of what he calls "The Prophet Movements."

We learn that in 1913 a wave of prophetism became strong in West Africa. On the Ivory Coast a certain "Prophet Harris" believed that he had been appointed by God in a vision to call men to repentance. This movement grew at a tremendous rate. It was estimated that in two years one hundred thousand people accepted allegiance to Harris. Presently unworthy "minor prophets" arose, whose only mission was to coin money out of the earnestness and credulity of the simple folk they "served." The government then asked Harris to leave that territory.

In 1921 a similar movement occurred in Lower Congo. It was a curious blend of Bible doctrine, legends, and superstition. The major prophet was one Kibangu, at one time a communicant member of a local church. In a dream Kibangu was commanded to preach and to heal. Thousands flocked to hear him, and large numbers of sick, blind, crippled,—even dead—were brought to him for treatment. He anointed the eyes of the blind with clay, and they believed they were healed, though their eyes were as opaque as ever. An African Christian, observing, said, "This business resembles the witchcraft of my fathers."

Prophet Kibangu's person was tabu—that is, sacred or inviolable. His "revelations" would "cause him to foam at the mouth and shake violently. Bible texts were quoted and misquoted." A medical missionary in the service of the American Mission Society stated that Kibangu was neurotic.

Further we are told that "men calling themselves prophets have been a recurring feature of Christian life in West Africa." The writer mentions one notorious prophet in particular, of whom he says, "In the meetings held by this man, prayer was made, the Bible was read, hymns were sung, and the end of the age announced. . . The prophet left disillusionment in his train. In many places Christian congregations were broken up, but in other places local village churches have arisen to the occasion and established daily classes for inquirers."

Later this movement left its original program of converting the heathen. Instead it began to effect the churches "so that there was danger of schism within some of them." In this respect they run true to type. Also the following is not unheard of among "prophets" in our own land: "Slogans against organized churches were later taken up by the prophet's followers, such as, 'The preacher should not be paid'; 'The churches seek only for money,'" "These things," says the writer, "linger in the minds of many people . . . and the danger is that some will leave a well-established, disciplined and instructed Church for bodies whose teaching and discipline are sub-Christian."

What shall we say? "What then brethren?" No doubt *some* true good comes out of even such a movement as this prophetism, be it in Africa or in America. But at what a price! Superstition, error, fanaticism, seem to be the beginning and the end of such religious cyclones. The spiritual atmosphere is cleared a little, but with a horrible trail of wreckage left behind. Though it may be that such prophetism is not identical with the modern tongues it most certainly is closely akin to it.

Enough, and more, of the tongues movement has now been rehearsed. Enough to show that the worldliness of the Corinthians, the imaginations of the Montanists, the fanaticism of the Zwickau prophets are duplicated in the Irvingites of the last century and in the pentecostals of today.

However, the most striking resemblance down through the ages is not the erratic behavior of individuals or of groups. Psychopathics we always have with us. Nor is the pronounced inclination to sensuality the most significant trait. Admittedly there are licentious men found within every denomination.

And yet, while admitted, there is *this vast difference:* the people not given to pentecostalism *do not defend nor condone fornication on the ground of spiritual superiority.* Such was the case in Corinth and has been the attitude of many tongue-talkers ever since. Even the most degenerate Romanist prelate of the Middle Ages never defended his immorality by saying: "The Spirit leads me to commit adultery—therefore it is right, for I am doing it in the Spirit!"

The most significant resemblance, and the heritage that seems to have passed from generation to generation and which we believe to be the most pernicious is the treacherous mirage of the pentecostal brand of rationalism!

Not that they are found in the ranks of "higher critics." Far from that. Yet they are ever prone to place their own "revelations" on par with God's Word, yes even superior to it. We are speaking the truth in love when we maintain that whenever fervently religious people hold the Scriptures to be an insufficient rule of life and conduct, they are rationalists, and the results will be utterly carnal.

Notice that the Corinthians were warned not "to go beyond the things which are written; that no one of you be puffed up" (I Cor. 4:6).

The Montanists "learned something more" from their leaders "than from the Law and the Prophets and the Gospels." The Zwickau prophets of Luther's day refused to "cling so closely to the Bible." The Irvingites denounced the Bible Societies.

And so often we find that a pentecostal today, regardless of what denomination he may be, is ready to declare as did one of their number: "I did not read the Bible for a year and a half after my baptism. I did not need to; the Spirit taught me. We are not in the time when we are living according to the Epistles yet, so what the Spirit leads us to do is right now."

Spiritual pride begets just such fundamental error. Such "going beyond what is written" in the search for light and joy always leads to spiritual darkness. And how great is that darkness!

Before closing this chapter, we want to add, in justice to true believers that are found in pentecostal denominations, that the fundamental doctrines of the Bible are taught in most of their churches. They who are on conservative ground are not always responsible for the frenzy of their radical brethren. Still, the very fact that even the more conservative of pentecostal folk do stress the *desirability* of ecstatic experiences is exactly what attracts many "seekers" from every communion and causes thousands to suffer shipwreck concerning the faith.

OCCASION AND CAUSE OF MODERN TONGUES

Pentecostal rationalism.

Mental instability.

Spiritual fever.

Mob psychology and hypnotism.

Demon power.

*O my people, they which lead thee cause thee to err,
and destroy the way of thy paths* (Isaiah 3:12b).

*I have heard what the prophets have said, that proph-
esy lies in my name, saying, I have dreamed, I have
dreamed. How long shall this be in the hearts of the
prophets that prophesy lies, even the prophets of the deceit of their own heart? that think to cause my people to
forget my name by their dreams which they tell every
man to his neighbor, as their fathers forgat my name for
Baal. The prophet that hath a dream, let him tell a
dream; and he that hath my word, let him speak my word
faithfully. What is the straw to the wheat? saith Jehovah.
Is not my word like fire? saith Jehovah; and like a ham-
mer that breaketh the rock in pieces? Therefore, behold,
I am against the prophets, saith Jehovah, that steal my
words every one from his neighbor. Behold, I am against
the prophets, saith Jehovah, that use their tongues, and
say, He saith. Behold, I am against them that prophesy
lying dreams, saith Jehovah, and do tell them, and cause
my people to err by their lies, and by their vain boasting;
yet I sent them not, nor commanded them; neither do
they profit this people at all, saith Jehovah* (Jeremiah
23:25-32).

*There is a conspiracy of her prophets in the midst
thereof, like a roaring lion ravening the prey: they have
devoured souls; they take treasure and precious things;
they have made her widows many in the midst thereof.
Her priests have done violence to my law, and have pro-
faned my holy things; they have made no distinction between the holy and the common, neither have they
caused men to discern between the unclean and the clean,
and have hid their eyes from my sabbaths, and I am pro-
faned among them* (Ezek. 22:25, 26).

CHAPTER SEVEN

Occasion and Cause of Modern Tongues

FREQUENTLY men conclude that the pentecostal movement must be of God because it spreads so rapidly among religious people. As if the popularity or the power of a religious movement were a guarantee of its divine origin and approval!

A fountain rises no higher than its source. A religious movement is no better than its basic doctrines. As already stated, most pentecostal sects are fundamentalists. But in spite of this, one finds in their theology just such errors that inevitably will "eat as doth a gangrene."

On the preceding pages we pointed to what we believe to be the most serious delusion of modern tongues. It is the disposition to subordinate Scripture to mere intuition and subjective experience. This, we are convinced, is not simply a prominent trait of pentecostalism. *It is the taproot from whence springs the entire growth.*

A lengthy doctrinal statement made by one of the larger pentecostal groups states in its concluding paragraph: "These are doctrines that were revealed from heaven and preached in the outpouring of the Spirit in Los Angeles, April, 1906." One may well ask: revealed from heaven to whom? If by this revelation they mean the Word of the Scriptures, why not say so plainly?

The claim of anyone to a direct and immediate inspiration or illumination *apart from the Word* whether it be by intense desire, or as the result of a passive receptivity, is unsound and un-Scriptural. We would underscore the following statement: "The theology of this 'gift of tongues' movement displays ignorance and perversion of Scripture. As already noticed, it subordinates the great facts and truths of the Christian revelation to the subjective experiences of the Christian life. But more than this, in its teaching about the Holy Spirit it subordinates what was primary and essential in Pentecost to what was incidental and altogether secondary. . . The Coming of the Holy Spirit is now as definitely a matter of fact as the Coming of the Son of God; and while to seek subjective proofs of His baptism as a condition of believing in it may be plausibly described as 'seeking a second Pentecost,' it is, in fact, sheer unbelief. It throws discredit upon that first and only true Pentecost, and calls in question the fulfillment of 'the promise of the Father.' " (Sir Robert Anderson.)

This type of intuitionism is the fundamental error of pentecostalism. There are contributory causes also. Perhaps they are more conspicuous. And just because they do attract attention, they are most effective agencies in the spread of this movement. Speaking of this movement as we observe it today, Alexander Mackie says in his book, *The Gift of Tongues,* "We have noticed that the manifestation of tongues has always begun with an individual in whom the presence of some disease can definitely be traced . . . There is every evidence pointing to the fact that the tongues are either a fraud or pathological or both."

Not infrequently do we hear that "too much religion makes people crazy." Such statements are due either to prejudice or to ignorance. The worldly world is always prejudiced against religion, that is if it is the religion which centers in the Christ of the Bible. Again, men ignorantly jump at the conclusion that the effect is the cause. It is not the Christian spiritual life in men, but the *suppression* of that life which may cause a mental upheaval. There are people whose mental health predispose them to such illness, much the same as some men are physically predisposed to certain bodily ailments.

The eminent mental specialist, Dr. Schou of Copenhagen, summarizes the statements of several of the most noted specialists in Europe, pertaining to this: "We may then venture to say that in the opinion of psychiatric authorities, religion, in the sense of a true and healthy attitude toward God, is not only harmless as regards mental health, but directly preservative."

In this connection we would also quote an American psychiatrist, Dr. Gordon B. Hamilton of Washington, D. C. An Associated Press dispatch quotes him with reference to increase of insanity, "In the past decade, and particularly in the past five years, the general level of sanity has gone down. Conversely, cases of inferiority complex, melancholia, neurasthenia, and psychoneuroses have increased sharply."

Whatever the cause of this serious situation, it makes one heavy-hearted to recall that at this very time pentecostalism also is on the increase. Can it be possible that the thousands of cases of neurasthenia, or nerve-weariness, or "nervous break-down" all about us, expose men and women to pentecostalism, while we remain in our "dispensaries" and prescribe a mere formal "service" as the remedy?

In any event the mental instability of some people indicates one of the avenues of pentecostalism. Most men who have studied this type of religious fervor agree that the movement is psychological as well as spiritual. This applies to individual cases, and it applies to groups.

In his book, *Religion and the Morbid Mental States,* Dr. Schou tells of numerous cases where a sick body and unbalanced mind combined to produce a pitifully morbid spiritual condition. The author cites instance after instance of such patients where the characteristic symptoms were "visions" and "voices" and incoherent talking while the patient was in a semi-conscious state or in a cataleptic condition.

Regarding the spasmodic and violent phases of the religious life in mentally unbalanced people, Dr. Schou says, "Religious life becomes . . . violent in psychosis (mental disease) . . . which may be suppressed in many people in every-day life." Further, "hallucinations are very common in cases of melancholia. The patients hear voices . . . they see visions in the forms of demons, flaming sword, and the like."

Medical men speak of one form of insanity as "reformatory, or religious paranoia." The patient believes that he is destined and appointed to abolish certain evils. Frequently such individuals suffer from what is known as *megalomania,* that is, an excessive idea of their own importance and greatness. Religious megalomania is frequently the real reason for schism and faction, and also for originating some new cult. Says Dr. Schou: "The slighter forms of religious paranoia are not uncommon, and often lie concealed among those persons who form new sects and congregations of their own, with some eccentric interpretation of the Bible. Little circles of this sort can do a great deal of harm, as for instance, by turning the heads of less intelligent persons."

The same author's description of the symptoms in one of his patients, further illustrates the problem. Of a young man he writes: "Owing to the morbid character of his religious life, he experienced a series of revelations, fell into mystic trances and saw visions, heard voices, etc., which produced a state of ecstasy for some time. . . . Simultaneously with these religious revelations he became entangled in a series of love affairs which seriously affected his strength, and ultimately placed him in the doctor's hands."

A paragraph pertaining to religious hysteria and the emotional life of hysterical persons in general is also most illuminating. "The last point of interest in hysteria from a religious and psychological point of view, which we must briefly mention here, is the peculiar character and unseen emotional life of these people, which we may comprise under the general term: hysterical constitution. It means that hysterical persons are ill-balanced, unreliable, impulsive, theatrical, anxious to draw attention to themselves, to 'make scenes,' and inclined to surprising explosive outbursts of feeling. . . . It is as if they must always overdo everything."

Now of course every reasonable person knows that the "speaking in tongues" or other traits of modern pentecostalism are not *necessarily* the outcome of such mental conditions as those just described, yet it seems to be demonstrated beyond a doubt that a weakened mind is a most suitable soil for such fanaticism. The groan of humanity, as of all creation, has been deep and long. Not loud always; often an undertone; oftener drowned in laughter, but still terribly real. If we realize that much of this groaning indicates a breaking mind as well as a burdened heart, we should sense it that such anguish of soul is beyond endurance.

Every pastor, though he may have had but little pastoral experience, has met with individuals who are melancholy, nervous, bewildered, psychopathic. Such persons may be as sincere seekers for peace with God as are their brothers with more stable disposition. Or, if he is a believer, he may be yearning for a closer walk with God.

Should we ignore or scoff at either of such desires? God forbid! What men in such spiritual crises need, is to be led firmly and dispassionately to see what God says in the Word.

When an unstable or eccentric person, in his search for light or for power, hears of some mysterious experiences of this man or that, he almost invariably hopes that some such strange things also may happen to him. His heart is set on this; his prayers center on it. The beatific "visions," the "being in the Spirit" that others claim as their lot he *must* have at whatever cost. He can not and will not take refuge in the plain promises of Christ, but must have some external sign or some inward ecstasy as proof of the "spirit-baptism."

If, then, he knows no rivers of living water flowing out from his life, if no thrill grips him, if no token appears, he is disappointed even unto despair. *He develops spiritual fever.* All because the mysterious "baptism" on which he had set his heart is sadly missing.

Because such a one is sick in soul—and, as we have seen, perhaps also in body and mind—he easily becomes the prey of religious quacks. They run to meet him with open arms. Also with many sanctimonious hints about the "regular" preachers and their "dead" churches. There are pious phrases about a "second blessing" and the need of "tarrying" for "the baptism." The process is usually more a "tearing" than a "tarrying." He keeps tearing around from one late meeting to the next until from sheer exhaustion he is ready for mental and spiritual collapse. The wearied and bewildered soul is then ushered into a circle of "workers" who are determined to see him "receive the baptism."

Do these "workers" point to the Lord Jesus as the author and perfector of faith? Do they direct the seeking soul to the Word which alone can make him wise unto salvation? No, all such is too commonplace, too dead!

Instead he is imperatively urged to "Yield! Yield! Get the baptism! Claim the Spirit!"

If these frantic suggestions from within and without fail to prostrate the victim, a special technique is applied. He is made to kneel, and then keep his arms raised heavenward. This exhausting position must be kept without interruption while he persistently "groans in the spirit" for signs to appear.

Of course, signs eventually do appear. The exhausted body and distracted mind must necessarily yield to the hypnotic method of the "workers." Then the contortions of body, the delirious ravings, the final stupor, are hailed as the "spirit baptism with signs!"

We have already described the results of such "tarrying," and shall refrain from further sordid details. The police of our large cities everywhere bear this testimony: "Continuously we are called to quiet disorder. We know beforehand what to find. Time and again we have found people completely 'out' in some back room as the result of the fanatical exercises."

Every one knows that human senses are effected by sudden or unexpected sensations. A flash of light, an explosive noise, a sharp pain, will startle us, and in a measure cause us to expect additional sensations. Certain kinds of revivalists are well aware of the technique of sudden sensation, though few will go to the length that we are told was used by some a few decades ago. They used to fire pistols at their meetings hoping that the sudden excitement caused in that way would create the desired state of mind.

The plan of leading up to a climax of "terrified sanctification," has been followed in more than one "holiness meeting." One must admit that there is method in their madness. It is much like the method of the Baal-priests on Mount Carmel, and though more effective, it is probably also more abominable in the sight of God.

That erratic and unhealthy expressions of religion will thrive where the spiritual life of the Church is at low ebb needs no proof. It was so in Israel of old; it is so even now. Therefore a sect-infested, diseased spirituality is a chastisement, yea, a judgment upon a lukewarm congregation.

We do need the breath of the Holy Spirit to revive the dry bones. But such quickening from on high is not granted as the result of any revival technique, nor in answer to a carnal demand for signs. Religious hysteria is frequently mistaken for fervent zeal. Yet its very nature is the opposite of a childlike trust in the promises of the Father.

It is altogether probable that should any pentecostal Christian chance to read these pages, he will say that this is all an unbeliever's way of rationalizing, and is evidence that the writer has never experienced the Spirit's baptism.

Now, if by "baptism" is meant either visions or tongues we plead guilty. However, an attorney is not required to break the law before he is permitted to deal with lawbreakers. A physician need not have contracted every human ill in order to diagnose a disease. Nor is it necessary for a servant of Christ to have been an infidel or a publican in order to recognize evidences of religious error. The apostle Paul was a moral man both before and after his conversion. And even though God granted to him the most extraordinary revelations, he found it not expedient to "glory" in those experiences. He says: "I would rather glory in my weaknesses, that the power of Christ may rest upon me."

God pity those who are "never able to come to the knowledge of the truth" (II Tim. 3:7)! They trust in shadowy fantasies and crave violent upheavals instead of the peace of God to guard their hearts and thoughts in Christ Jesus. They cheat themselves with a play at Bible phrases. They cheat themselves with an occasional picnic-lunch happiness, and know not how to rejoice always in Him who is the Bread of Life. They seek perfection in their own imperfect "surrendering," and unwittingly reject the believer's perfection in Christ. They profess to honor the Spirit by defiling His temple; or they proceed to "crucify the flesh" by torturing the body.

There is also a less-serious-minded type of people drawn to the meetings of tongue-talkers for a somewhat different reason. They are the thrill-chasers, the seekers after radicalism. They relish anything and everything sensational whether in politics, in business, in society, or in church. That which is orderly is far too drab for them. Their religious life is superficial, not deep; contentious, not contented.

Of course, where the carcasses are, there will the vultures be gathered. There never was a scarcity of "missionaries" eager to minister to the excitables.

The sensation-seekers get supreme satisfaction in hearing harangues on the most hair-raising subjects. Certain favorite "prophetic" texts are construed so as to fit any current tragedy. The singing savors of religious jazz. The "message" abounds in sulphuric stories of revelations and signs. In short, the stage is set for a three-ring religious circus; side-show, fire-eaters, and lion-tamers included!

Frequently it happens then, that they who came in order to be entertained and to have cold chills of excitement running up and down their spines, themselves become the center of attraction. That is in itself a great satisfaction. Every emotional reaction experienced at such a "full-gospel service" is to them an evidence of sanctification. At least it affords occasion later, to tell the members of "dead" churches how wonderful it is to go to the lively ones.

Is it at all surprising that men and women, ignorant, baffled, and mystified, are caught under such circumstances? They are ensnared in the meshes of mass-hypnotism. They readily respond to the invitation to "come forward" and to "seek the baptism." The very atmosphere is charged with emotional expectancy. Something must happen.

Mob psychology comes into play. All about, there are men and women groaning, screaming, prostrate on the floor, while others jubilantly jump up and down at "the spirit's presence." Presently there is a chattering voice heard in a corner, soon more gibberish in another; now several are seized by the lalomania, and general pandemonium reigns.

Sign-seekers soon find themselves overcome in such surroundings. What else is to be expected? Indeed it takes exceptional mental vigor and spiritual stamina to withstand the powerful, preter-human spirit of the place.

Anyone who has experimented with mesmerism even in the most amateurish fashion, knows how they who play the game unconsciously yield to the suggestions of the leader. What then, where everything is effectively set to bring about a response? Religious charlatanry has a tremendous power. The strong sign-fixation present makes them easy victims of the delusions.

Why do men seek and accept spiritual advice that invariably leads to confusion and disaster?

Neither Paul nor Peter ever exhorted their followers to persist in looking for spectacular evidences of holiness. Their desire was that men be looking unto Jesus! Neither tongues nor hysteria is counted as the fruits of the Spirit. Love, and self-control, are the first and the last of this fruit (Gal. 5:22-23).

How great is the darkness in men, whose first aspirations were to be truly "filled unto all the fulness of God" if the spirit of pentecostalism converts such ideals into a carnal desire for personal gratification and display! The most saintly humility and the most severe self-abasement are then "of no value against the indulgence of the flesh." The most ardent zeal in such a one is merely another sort of work-righteousness, a man-begotten work-holiness.

Sincere men and women say that they can not describe their experience when first speaking in tongues. They testify that it is "too wonderful for words." We believe that is true. We also believe that in tongues they had a "real religious experience."

But not every wonderful feeling, nor every real religious experience is from God! Far from it!

We stated in a previous chapter that speaking in tongues and its accompanying symptoms were known in the ancient pagan world. However such demoniacal infillings and manifestations are not limited to the heathen of the Orient of two thousand years ago. As an instance of such phenomena in our day a report from Greenland is worthy of note. A book, recently published, is *Arctic Adventure* (New York, 1935), written by one Peter Freuchen. The author is a Dane who, because of disappointments decided to leave European civilization and to "go native" among the Eskimos of Greenland. This he did to the limit. He joined a tribe that is still pagan, or nearly so. He married an Eskimo woman. He joined the natives in their work and in their worship. After many years as an Eskimo he returned to civilization and wrote the book of his Arctic adventures.

In one chapter the author tells of a series of calamities that befell the tribe to which he belonged. The "angakok" (or medicine man or priest) named Sorgaa, prepared to get in touch with the spirits of the nether world to ascertain the reasons for their wrath.

The Danish adventurer decided to attend the medicine

man's "service," and took part in the procedure. The priest's assistant was in charge of the preparations. "His eyes burned with fervor, his gestures were quick, his walk nervous."

At first the angakok tried to dissuade the white man from being present at the rites, saying "This is nothing for a man like you to look at. I am only a big liar, and even if these idiots are stupid enough to believe me, I never expected you to stand for it. I am only a foolish old man, and what happens here has nothing to do with the truth."

The mystic rites were performed in a large igloo draped with tapestry of old skins. The place was filled with men and women tense with expectation. The writer says, "I was intoxicated by the heat and the odor of bodies and the song. . . . All of us sat there singing as we had before. Ecstasy was upon the face of every man and woman. Their cheeks were swollen, their eyes bright and shining. Their mouths hung open and their bodies were naked from the waist up to endure the heat. They swayed back and forth to the rhythm of the song . . . no one seemed to see anything."

"In the middle of the floor was Krilerneq (the priest's assistant) writhing and twisting like a dancer. Beside me sat a young girl, Ivaloo. Her naked body was pressed against mine, and her strong, young scent swept over me. . . . The rhythmic swish of her hair made me as senseless as the rest of them."

". . . When I looked into the faces of these people I could scarcely recognize them as the calm, quiet friends who come down to Thule to trade with us. . . Here I saw them caught up by a spirit which they could not possibly understand, the prey to emotions and passions which in everyday life would puzzle them."

"Suddenly one of the men, Krisuk, went out of his head.

Unable to contain himself to the regular rhythm of the service he leapt to his feet crying like a raven and howling like a wolf. In ecstasy he and the girl, Ivaloo, began to yell in a tongue I could not understand . . . certainly it was not the usual Eskimo language . . . *and if there is such a thing as speaking in tongues I heard it then."* (Page 135. Italics are ours.)

"The song continued and I fell completely under the power of the spirit. No longer was I able to observe dispassionately what occurred. . . The noise, the odor of bodies, and the mystery of the moment caught me completely unprepared. . . The igloo reverberated with the noise of his (the priest's) drum. . . I raised my hand to grasp the skin (that draped the walls) and received such a blow on my arm that the bone was almost shattered. Hell itself had suddenly come to earth."

Speaking of the close of this religious orgy, the author says of the priest, "He sat quietly . . . then fell back and lay in a coma. At last he opened his eyes. His voice was weak and his mouth dry. He tried to smile as he saw me. 'Just lies and bunk the whole thing!' he said. 'Do not believe in anything. I am no angakok. I speaking nothing but lies'."

No comment is necessary. Some of the sordid details of the narrative have been omitted. From beginning to end this tongue-talking "service" by the natives of Greenland is an exact duplication of the spirit and behavior of tongue-talking cults in our own country. The Eskimos did not accredit their orgies to the Spirit of God, for Him they did not know. They attributed the ecstasy to the devil, to whom it rightly belongs.

There is a power, not human, but far stronger than human, to be reckoned with. There is something more effective than all mental suggestion and hypnotic influence combined. A power that can becloud the keenest human intellect. That is the power of Satan.

Some "New Thought,"—or shall we say, very old thought—folk are through with the devil. He is only a grotesque scare-crow handed down from the dark ages. And behold! Because these scintillating new-thinkers *deny* the devil's existence, therefore he does not exist! Such is the logic of unbelief!

It is good form for all such intellectualists to ascribe any and all spiritual aberrations to mental or physical inadequacy. The spiritual does not exist. In their superiority they do not deign even to hold in contempt that which pertains to the realm of spirits. If, forsooth, there be some "helpful discourse" offered by a Reader, a Medium, or some other faking Fakir, all such common-place words as spirit, or matter, or angel, or demon, require a dictionary-definition all its own in order to be acceptable. This very attitude on the part of some people would indicate that some power not their own has blinded their minds. One can account for their position only in terms of spirit influence.

Whether admitted or denied, Satan does exist. He does wield his power among men. Some he keeps asleep with mental opiates. Others he prods along with psychic stimulants. No doubt, it matters little to the Prince of darkness by what means sinners are kept in bondage just so they remain there.

Scripture teaches that there is an unseen, yet very real world of spirits round about us. There are principalities and powers contending for the possession and rule of men. Evil spirits are about their prince's business just as surely as are the holy angels ministering to those who shall inherit salvation.

Devout people within the church need to remember this. Prove the thrills, the sensations, the mysteries, the spirits, whether they be of God. Satan will readily give spiritual experiences when it serves his purpose. Demons will not object even to be driven out of men, for even that can be turned to the favor of the father of lies. (Matt. 12:45.) The very excitement of exorcism he will use to draw men's attention away from Jesus Christ.

Man also has his spirit. He is not a beast of the field. He is human. It is because of this that spirits from without are able to make *spiritual* contact with man. The human spirit either responds to the approach of the other, or else rejects and opposes such contact.

Our readers should realize that when the Bible speaks of demons, they are not phantasies or imaginary influences. They are real; yet so hidden from human understanding that their existence is indistinctly realized. However, many a faithful saint of God does realize and recognize this adversary. To Paul, the prince of the power of the air was as distinct and real as was Tertullus or Nero.

The limitations of the material world seem to disappear in the realm of spirits. Countless are the cases where physical and intellectual giants have become helpless victims of an evil spirit. On the other hand, countless are also the times when men, strong in their own prowess, yielded to the Holy Spirit and were transformed into obedient children of God. Consequently man may be led by the Spirit of God, or he may be dominated by a stronger human mind, or he may be used by a spirit of Satan.

Whenever the Holy Spirit would do His work in the hearts of men, the devil is prepared to offer his substitutes. His wares are attractive to natural man. If he can gain his end in no other way he will appear as an angel of light, that is, as a messenger from God. Arrayed in what closely resembles truth, he accomplishes and sustains his deceptions. His speech is Scripture-flavored, his deeds are wonderful works in Jesus' Name, his signs are marvelous counterfeits of the Holy Spirit's ministry.

"Satan sets forth and decks all his words and works with the color of truth and with the Name of God." Yes, he will imitate the Holy Spirit if thereby he may draw men away from Christ. To defeat Christ in the Church is his aim and goal.

Not a few sincere people are over-awed at the thought of a miracle, or what may appear to be a miracle. They forget that such signs, be they ever so genuine, are not always from God. We have stressed this fearful truth in a previous chapter, but the lesson bears repetition. In the first book of the Bible we are told how man was first deceived by the devil. In the last book of the Bible there is the prediction and description of spirits of demons *working signs*. (Rev. 16:14.)

"A miracle," says Sir Robert Anderson, "is an event which gives proof of the operation of some supernatural agency. And Spiritualism and Christian Science can boast of real miracles. Hence the marvelous advance that these cults are making in our day. For what wins to them adherents among the devout is not the element of imposture which leavens them, but the spiritual power by which they are seemingly accredited. For . . . people assume as a matter of course that miracles must be divine."

The Bible tells us repeatedly of wicked men who performed wonderful works. That is, the deeds were wonderful because apparently done by supernatural power. We read of the magicians of Egypt who so strangely imitated Moses; the amazing reputation of Simon the sorcerer as "that power of God which is called Great," the magic arts of Elymas on the Isle of Cyprus.

Usually such men brazenly tell a lie about their errand as did the old prophet in Bethel when he deceived and destroyed one of God's servants, saying, "An angel spake

unto us by the word of Jehovah . . . but he lied unto him."
(I Kings 13:18.) At other times, however, false prophets
are used by God in bringing judgment upon men who
persist in unbelief. "Now therefore, behold, Jehovah hath
put a lying spirit in the mouth of all these thy prophets;
and Jehovah hath spoken evil concerning thee" (I Kings
22:23). Surely if men persistently choose to believe a lie,
the Lord will at last send just such a judgment upon
them. It will be even to them according to their faith.

False prophets and false wonder-workers have constantly infested the Church. They speak in the Name of
Jesus even when driving out demons, but the evil spirits
are no more afraid of them than they were of the strolling
Jews of Ephesus (Acts 19:13). Yes, though the unclean
spirits themselves speak the Name of Jesus, they are unclean spirits nevertheless. The evangelists tell us that
Christ permitted not the demons to speak, even though
they knew Him and spoke the truth about Him.

But why point out the power and deceitfulness of
demons in this discussion? Because the demons who thus
can and will impersonate the Holy Spirit can also cause
men to speak words that are not mind-controlled, and to
utter sounds that are beyond human reason.

The awful fact in this connection is that *the evil spirits
spoke through men*. Those men were not raving maniacs
in every instance. We find them even in the synagogues,
where they behaved much like other men, until confronted
by Christ Himself. Then it was that in their hellish hatred
to Christ the demons took possession of the vocal organs
of their victims. Thus, by the direct power of the devil,
were human tongues made to utter *holy words* in defiance
of Christ!

Pertaining to this we call attention to what the eminent
Dutch theologian, the late Dr. Kuyper, says about speaking in tongues. "This is not due to man's thinking but in

consequence of an entirely different operation. That this is possible we see, first, in delirious persons who say things outside of their own personal thinking; second, in the insane, whose incoherent talk has no sense; third, in persons possessed, whose vocal organs are used by demons. . . Hence it must be concluded . . . that the use of these (vocal) organs may be appropriated by a spirit who has overcome him."

Anyone who has heard the unnatural ring of authority in the voice of some pentecostal leader in charge of a frenzied tongues-session will never forget the weird impression. One seems to sense a power, well-nigh irresistible, in the tenseness of the voice, that makes one shudder with apprehension. It seems that evil spirits find demoniacal joy in betraying men, in contrast to the joy of angels in heaven when a sinner repents.

Are we now as they who call in question every expression of spiritual power? Or are we uncharitable and unjust in attributing much of tongue-talking ability to the direct work of Satan? Do not even pentecostal people do the same?

Out of their own mouths shall they be judged. Says H. A. Ironside, whom we previously quoted: "Lately divisions have been rife among the Pentecostal people, and the adherents of the various parties roundly anathemize one another, *but they all have the same marvelous sign* of speaking in 'tongues.' Each party declares the 'tongues' are of the devil when found among their adversaries, but inveighs solemnly against all who dare question their own peculiar gift being of the Holy Spirit."

In concluding the chapter on man-produced and demon-produced signs, we once more call attention to what is written in God's Word. "But the Spirit saith expressly, that in later times some shall fall away from the faith, giving heed to seducing spirits and doctrines of demons, through the hypocrisy of men that speak lies, branded in their own conscience as with a hot iron" (I Tim. 4:1-2). Truly, "our wrestling is not against flesh and blood, but against the principalities, against the powers, against the world-rulers of this darkness, against the spiritual hosts of wickedness in the heavenly places" (Eph. 6:12).

THE CESSATION OF TONGUES

The Church is historic.

The Church is still apostolic.

Cessation of tongues and prophecies.

Scriptural inspiration completed.

Miracles, past and present.

Love never faileth: but whether there be prophecies, they shall be done away; whether there be tongues, they shall cease; whether there be knowledge, it shall be done away. For we know in part, and we prophesy in part: but when that which is perfect is come, that which is in part shall be done away. When I was a child, I thought as a child: now that I am become a man, I have put away childish things (I Cor. 13:8-11).

Why will ye be still stricken, that ye revolt more and more? the whole head is sick, and the whole heart faint. From the sole of the foot even unto the head there is no soundness in it; but wounds, and bruises, and fresh stripes: they have not been closed, neither bound up, neither mollified with oil (Isaiah 1:5, 6).

And every one that heareth these words of mine, and doeth them not, shall be likened unto a foolish man, who built his house upon the sand: And the rain descended, and the floods came, and the winds blew, and smote upon that house; and it fell: and great was the fall thereof (Matt. 7:26, 27).

Howbeit the firm foundation of God standeth, having this seal, The Lord knoweth them that are his: and, Let every one that nameth the name of the Lord depart from unrighteousness (II Tim. 2:19).

So then ye are no more strangers and sojourners, but ye are fellow-citizens with the saints, and of the household of God, being built upon the foundation of the apostles and prophets, Christ Jesus himself being the chief corner stone; in whom each several building, fitly framed together, groweth into a holy temple in the Lord; in whom ye also are builded together for a habitation of God in the Spirit (Eph. 2:19-22).

CHAPTER EIGHT

The Cessation of Tongues

THE life of Christianity is more than Church History; it is Christ. Yet it also is historical. We are creatures of time and must take into account the development of the Christian Church from generation to generation.

Probably this will not get us far in our contact with men and women of the pentecostal type. They do not heed historical facts. All such are to them but "the letter that killeth." But mature men and women of leadership in our evangelical churches will profit by having an historical perspective of Christianity. And young Christians will be stabilized in their loyalty to the faith of their fathers when they learn that this faith is "living still."

The Church must not forget her origin. In her historical records and historic experience she is ever linked to her Lord, who in the fulness of time became flesh and dwelt amongst us. That coming is not a wish nor a theory; it is an historic fact. Then, too, the historic Church alone understands the current religious movements, for her history contains many parallels of that which some take to be an entirely new feature.

It has always been a trait in fanatical movements to ignore and even deny the continuity of Christianity. The development of centuries is regarded virtually as a total failure. In the endeavor to create truly "apostolic" churches, they attempt to connect directly with the apostolic era. Without the slightest regard for local conditions in the Bible lands of Bible times, they will imitate literally the external features of the Church of that day.

The acts of the apostles are sought repeatedly. It is expected that current events of the present time forthwith shall be recognized and proclaimed as the actual recurrence of what took place nineteen hundred years ago. Of course, the result is a grotesque literalism in Bible interpretation and a slavish legalism in its application.

Christians must realize that the Church is still on earth, and that it is human as well as divine, temporal as well as spiritual. The Church is a living organism, but it has the form of an organization. The prophecies that *are* fulfilled and events that *are* past are not to be repeated in God's economy. It knows only one Pentecost as it knows only one Good Friday. It does not expect a repetition of the revelation to Paul in Arabia nor to John on Patmos. They were special and completed events, not only in the lives of those men but also in the life of the Church of Christ.

The work of the Holy Spirit is never magical nor mechanical. Even in the Old Testament eras His ministrations were in some manner connected with His Word, direct or symbolic, quite frequently both. And because that which is supernatural is of necessity different from the ordinary, it does occur more plainly during extraordinary times; especially at those creative periods when some providential epoch has its beginning. The very first verse in the Bible has in it the element of time. Though God is eternal, He takes account of time in His dealing with men. Some day we shall experience that "time is no more" but that is yet to come.

True believers will honor the Apostolic Church. It will always be the Church's ideal as well as its beginning. Still, we must not suppose that the life of that day can forthwith be duplicated in our own time. A past era can not and shall not be repeated. That would be contrary to

God's plan and providence. We humans cannot avoid our own day, nor can we sever connection with the day of our fathers.

The apostle Paul touches upon this truth in his discourse on the Corinthian tongues. He is himself a subject of time. When he was a child he was like other children. And when he reached maturity he did not revert to childhood; still he was the same human being. So likewise there are certain abiding things in the Church, and certain things that were destined to pass.

"Tongues shall cease." This gift served its purpose as a sign from God in the Church's childhood. One of pentecostal persuasion may ask: Why should "prophecies be done away" and "tongues cease," while many of the other grace-gifts continue? Our answer is: We only know what God says in His Word. He has chosen not always to give reasons for His all-wise rule in the Church. Furthermore we know, as stated repeatedly, that tongues *have* ceased; that is, such tongues that are from God.

We would heartily and humbly acknowledge that pentecostals of every era have sent forth well-deserved rebukes to a superficial Church. But a whip is not justified in becoming a scorpion. "I have heard what the prophets have said, that prophesy lies in my name, saying, I have dreamed, I have dreamed. . . . Behold, I am against them that prophesy lying dreams, saith Jehovah, and do tell them, and cause my people to err by their lies, and by their vain boasting: yet I sent them not, nor commanded them; neither do they profit this people at all, saith Jehovah" (Jer. 23:25, 32). The very fact that certain tongues have appeared periodically after the days of Paul would indicate that they were of another spirit, because they persist contrary to the Word.

Perhaps few Bible scholars will say with absolute finality that the Holy Spirit has never once, anywhere, mani-

fested His presence in tongues later in the Christian era.
God may have seen fit to repeat certain signs at times and
in places where He chose to do so. Of this we shall speak
presently.

However, we have the best of reasons to question the
genuineness of most post-apostolic signs. We do so
because God has said they shall cease. And also because
of the un-Scriptural, unholy, unspeakable fruits of the
tongues movement everywhere. By their fruits we know
them.

Furthermore, "prophecies shall be done away." Not
the form of "prophecy" which consists chiefly in preaching and teaching the Word of God. That method of gath-
ering disciples into the Church shall continue; all the New
Testament tells us that. But the kind of "prophecy" which
consisted largely, if not entirely, in foretelling and future-
telling should cease. It was a mystic form of inspired testimony based largely on direct revelation. That has been
done away.

Both forms of prophecy were known in the early Church.
The Old and New Testament are "the Word of prophecy." The writing of these Scriptures was finished in the
first century. Since *that* form of prophecy was taken away
just as soon as Christendom had received the completed
Bible, it is neither un-Scriptural nor strange to say that
tongues likewise ceased as soon as the written Word had
been delivered to the Church. Thereafter the members of
the Church should rely altogether on that Book, and no
supplementary sign or revelation was needed. If men
would refuse to accept the Word, neither would they
believe if someone produced supernatural signs.

The apostolic Christians believed and taught that God
had "of old time spoken unto the fathers in the prophets
by divers portions and in divers manners." They knew
also the writing of the Old Testament Scriptures as an

accomplished fact. In addition to this they recognized that after a silence of four hundred years God spoke "unto us in His Son."

The early post-apostolic Church had the same convictions. They realized that when Christ had come and His Church was being planted, a new era, a creative epoch in religion had come. They also knew that *laying the foundation is one thing* but *continuing to build thereon is something else.* The theory of a continuous revelation was rejected by them. "They believed that the inspiration which indited the Holy Scriptures was unique." That certainty has been the strength of the Church in all ages.

Bishop Lightfoot says: "The reception of the gospels by the early Church was immediate and universal. They were never placed for a moment in the same category with spurious documents which soon sprang up after them. . . . though in some cases bearing the name and pretending to contain the teaching of an apostle."

The early Church Fathers thought and wrote in an atmosphere of Christian experience. Their theology was not hurriedly made to order so that they might offer something "different." It was "graven on their hearts and on the palms of their hands." To belittle or ignore this is "sheer spiritual conceitedness." "For such men are false apostles, deceitful workers, fashioning themselves into apostles of Christ." The Church is not to bear with them but to "try them that call themselves apostles, and they are not." We have the unerring written Word in its completeness, accessible everywhere. The disciples who lived during the first decades of Christianity did not have that. We have the accumulated experience of the Lord's saints these many centuries. Though at times they were but a "remnant," yet were they faithful. Shall we utterly despise that heritage?

In spite of all evidence to the contrary, there are some who claim that direct, supernatural inspiration still continues. That doctrine has a hopeless sequence. If divine revelation were never completed, it follows that God's Word as we have it is incomplete, insufficient, and unreliable. Then is Peter's statement: "We have the Word of Prophecy made more sure," a falsehood! Then are we, who have looked to the Christ of that Word, of all men most deluded! Then are we stranded on the shoals of the most subtle kind of rationalism, which adds to, or subtracts from, the Bible as it seems convenient.

It was stated above that there may possibly have been times and places for supernatural signs also in later eras. For instance, where the Gospel is just being introduced and where the ordinary use of the Word is so unheard of and so little understood that the Lord permits extraordinary signs to accompany His messengers. We have not learned of authentic instances of this kind; we only hold that such possible exceptions would not contradict the intent of the apostle's statement.

Aside from such mere possibilities, we are firmly convinced that tongues have ceased. What else does Paul mean? The absurd interpretation that "tongues shall cease in heaven" is not even worthy of mention. The apostle foretold and history has verified that the supernatural gifts have "ceased more and more as the Christian Church more and more developed on the historical basis of revelation as completed in Christ."

In this connection, the Reverend W. Graham Scroggie also says: "It is most important to observe that one age does not end before the next begins but that they overlap one another, and that the period of this overlapping is in each instance a transition period with its peculiar characteristics. The signs wrought in Egypt immediately preceding Israel's release have their parallel in the signs wrought during the apostolic period which ushered in the present econômy. Let us remember that at the time of which we are speaking there was no New Testament to which appeal could be made, and for this reason, in part, no doubt, signs were vouchsafed them as evidences of the Divine presence and power. . . The present is not an age of sensuous signs, but of spiritual power, and if, for lack of experience of that power, we resort to what is sensuous, we need not be surprised that the devil makes the most of the opportunity."

God expects His children to grow and to develop. They are to begin with "the doctrine of the first principles of Christ," but not to stop at that. They shall "not lay again a foundation," but press on unto perfection (Heb. 6:1).

So does the Holy Spirit also direct the progress of the Church of Christ. When the foundation has been laid, the work shall not cease. It shall continue on that foundation, not as foundation-work but as work on the superstructure. Yes, more than that, there shall on the part of the builders be a constant looking forward to the glorious consummation of the work, the Church triumphant. The Church was given the inspired Word, the Bible. After the completed revelation the special prophetic gift was discontinued; it was "done away." That special enduement is no longer required.

So far from being evidence of retrogression on the part of the Church, the cessation of tongues, and also of other external signs, are proof of the very opposite. *We recognize therein a true development, an evidence of progress.* For it would be strange if the work in building a superstructure were on the same level as the laying of a foundation.

Perhaps one other religious factor also should be mentioned from the historical viewpoint. We have in mind the working of miracles to which we so often have alluded.

Every thinking Christian has been confronted with what one might call an absence of miracles in our day. And not in our generation alone, but practically since the days of the apostles. This is a bewildering, baffling situation to some people, and accounts for the popularity of any man or woman who can "produce the goods," that is, perform miracles. That immediately makes them "apostolic" in the eyes of a curious humanity.

Perhaps it were better if we recognized divine providence also here, and saw that in this too, God's method is not the same when He begins a work as it is after the work is under way. The purpose is the same, though the plan is different as ages and dispensations differ.

The faithful leaders of Christianity in the early centuries recognized this. Chrysostom, who lived in the fourth century writes regarding this difference between the time of the apostles and his own. "Miracles were wrought also among the Jews when wandering in the wilderness; . . . among us too, when we had just come out of error many wonderful works were shown forth, *but afterwards they stayed,* when in all countries true religion had taken root." Further on we note that imitation of apostolic miracles was regarded "as the attempt to employ evil, occult powers."

In his book *The Post-Apostolic Age* Dr. Remensnyder says: "Miracles are necessary to the introduction of a new epoch in the kingdom of God. Consequently, we do not find them of continuous occurrence. But they are sent to inaugurate the epoch, and when that is sufficiently authenticated, they are withdrawn. The supernatural is only employed for the extraordinary; the necessity disappearing, the natural order resumes sway."

"Accordingly, the two great cycles in the history of the kingdom of God, the leading forth of the Israelites to begin the history of a divine revelation, and the founding of Christianity, were the periods of the most wonderful breaking forth of miracles."

"Miracles would cease to be such if they were made a regular and ordinary mode. And if they were to break forth, occasionally here and there, endless opportunity would be afforded for fraud, and Christian history would be thrown into disorder and confusion. Hence, miracles ceased at a very definite time. The apostolic period over, Christianity being sufficiently authenticated, its propagation is thenceforth to be without this visible supernatural intervention."

We have now discussed miracles as they were granted in certain epochs, wherein they were of such prevalence and power that they had a marked influence upon their times.

Every Bible reader knows that during the ages of the first advent there were, as far as we can learn, some eras characterized by numerous miracles and other eras when they were practically unknown.

All believers agree that the God of Noah, of Moses, of Elijah, of Daniel, of Peter and Paul, is still the same today. He can and will reveal His omnipotence whenever and wherever He chooses. He does so reveal Himself frequently where the still, small voice of the Written Word is as yet nearly unknown. Of course, "for the indifferent there are no miracles. It is only the religious souls who are capable of recognizing the finger of God in certain given facts."

Therefore, all present-day miracles are not denied. Nor is it implied that all are wrought by evil powers. "No one may limit what God will do in response to faith. But we may dogmatically assert that, in view of the revelation He has given of Himself in Christ, He will yield nothing to the petulant demands of unbelief." (Sir R. Anderson.)

Our concern in this case is not to circumscribe the power of God. Neither is it to condemn every one, whose spiritual experiences do not coincide with our own. Our attitude must be to pray that prayer of our fathers: "Come Holy Spirit, Heavenly Dove, with *all* Thy quickening power!"

At the same time we also would watch, lest we be deluded by the wonders of the Wicked One. Satan's signs and wonders of falsehood may at first appear as refreshing showers but will soon become a deluge of confusion.

We have given considerable space to the historic phase of the problems connected with supernatural signs because we believe the situation warrants it. Not indeed that to history, nor to historic development has been given the office or power to modify the Word, but to make it more distinct and available first to human faith and then to human understanding.

"If the foundations be destroyed, what can the righteous do?" If the Church is not that of the Apostles and their contemporaries it is not the Christian Church. Then have the gates of hell already prevailed against it! Then was Christ mistaken when He said of the workmen in His Church: "Greater works than these shall he do." Greater, not in the rule of wind and wave, nor in calling forth men out of their graves, but greater works through Christ and for Christ when used by His Holy Spirit to preach that Word which makes men new creatures in Christ.

So long as the Bride of Christ is here on earth face-to-face communion with her Bridegroom is withheld. But her heart may communicate with her Lord, imperfect though that communication will be; and she may read the letters of love which He has sent to her. Until the day of the marriage feast of the Lamb, the letters from God, the written Word of God, remains the indispensible instrument by which believers are prepared for their future glory.

> *The Church from her dear Master*
> *Received the Gift divine*
> *And still that light she lifteth*
> *O'er all the earth to shine.*
> *It is the golden casket*
> *Where gems of truth are stored,*
> *It is the heav'n-drawn picture*
> *Of Christ, the living Word.*
>
> *It floateth like a banner*
> *Before God's hosts unfurled;*
> *It shineth like a beacon*
> *Above the darkling world:*
> *It is the chart and compass*
> *That o'er life's surging sea,*
> *'Mid mists and rocks and quicksands,*
> *Still guides, O Christ, to Thee.*
>
> *O make Thy Church, dear Savior,*
> *A lamp of burnished gold*
> *To bear before the nations*
> *Thy true light as of old:*
> *O teach Thy wandering pilgrims*
> *By this their path to trace,*
> *Till, clouds and darkness ended,*
> *They see Thee face to face.*

(W. W. Howe)

THE APPROACH TO THE PROBLEM

Speaking truth in love.
Persecution does not check error.
Whatsoever He saith unto you.
The precepts in First Corinthians
Forbid not.

We can do nothing against the truth, but for the truth (II Cor. 13:8).

These things saith the Amen, the faithful and true witness, the beginning of the creation of God: I know thy works, that thou art neither cold nor hot: I would thou wert cold or hot. So because thou art lukewarm, and neither hot nor cold, I will spew thee out of my mouth (Rev. 3:14b-16).

For I am jealous over you with a godly jealousy: for I espoused you to one husband, that I might present you as a pure virgin to Christ (II Cor. 11:2).

Besides those things that are without, there is that which presseth upon me daily, anxiety for all the churches. Who is weak, and I am not weak? who is caused to stumble, and I burn not? If I must needs glory, I will glory in the things that concern my weakness (II Cor. 11:28-30).

Therefore seeing we have this ministry, even as we obtained mercy, we faint not: but we have renounced the hidden things of shame, not walking in craftiness, nor handling the word of God deceitfully; but by the manifestation of the truth commending ourselves to every man's conscience in the sight of God. And even if our gospel is veiled, it is veiled in them that perish: in whom the god of this world hath blinded the minds of the unbelieving, that the light of the gospel of the glory of Christ, who is the image of God, should not dawn upon them (II Cor. 4:1-4).

Thus saith Jehovah, thy Redeemer, the Holy One of Israel: I am Jehovah thy God, who teacheth thee to profit, who leadeth thee by the way that thou shouldest go. Oh that thou hadst hearkened to my commandments! then had thy peace been as a river, and thy righteousness as the waves of the sea (Isaiah 48:17,18).

CHAPTER NINE

The Approach to the Problem

NOW the question arises concerning our attitude to the problem of pentecostalism. Or rather, what shall be our approach in dealing with it? We would emphasize immediately that our approach must not be headfirst, but heartfirst. Not headfirst either in plunging hastily into the fray, or headfirst in that we look to cold intellect to point the way. But heartfirst, realizing that very many of those concerned are bewildered children; and heartfirst, in that the love of Christ constrains us to love the erring enough to expose the errors.

Before proceeding further a review and restatement of the problem may not be amiss. When we now discuss the approach, and in the concluding chapter shall speak of the remedy, we do not thereby imply that the "last word" has been spoken on pentecostalism.

Pentecostalism is not the problem of certain sects or organized denominations. We stated this at the very outset; we emphasize it now. Hence the difficulty is not as easily localized as some may think. In fact it is not localized at all. All sects are more or less confined to territorial bounds, being more numerous in some localities than in others. Not so with pentecostalism.

The mental attitude and spiritual tendency which characterize this religious movement is both subtle and widespread. It is a challenge to every true disciple to more prayer, more Bible knowledge, more spiritual enlightenment, more zeal for Christ. Then too, we want to remind ourselves that the power and methods of pentecostalism are more subtle than mysterious. Much of its mystery disappears when we consider one of its sources, that which is the real source of all error and confusion among men. This movement is subtle because it is satanic. That is the verdict of the Scriptures. It is verified by the horrid trail of schism, immorality and insanity that everywhere has marked its inroads into the Church.

Many sincere people are entangled in this form of religious delusion. That must grieve us the most deeply. Not only are the carnal minded blindfolded thereby, but such who seek for peace of heart are misled, and the pious are bewildered. It is difficult to discern the spirit of such a religious movement because the counterfeit is so amazingly like the genuine. Men who become pentecostals are not agnostics nor materialists. Usually they are religious folks. They yearn for spiritual experience, and then because of neglect on the one hand and aggressiveness on the other, they soon are spiritually adrift. Such persons must be taught, not taunted; they must be directed, not denounced. We need especially to be "speaking truth in *love*" when we attempt to help those who are caught by the wiles of error.

When a tent has been pitched in the community we need not wait long till reports come of the "large assembly," the "marvelous speaker" and the "wonderful spirit in the meetings." All this may be true. That this is no infallible proof of the Holy Spirit's presence need not be repeated.

It happens not infrequently that when we get such reports and are confronted with such a situation we become both indignant and zealous. It is not always a righteous indignation, nor a holy zeal. Sometimes the indignation is much akin to that caused by an alarm clock, and the zeal is that of a hunter rather than that of a shepherd.

There is grave danger that we become negative only, in our entire attitude toward pentecostalism and every other ism. But negativism is not equivalent to orthodoxy. Neither is a contentious person the most valiant contender for the faith. His stand is as frequently due to cowardice as it is to courage, and instead of giving reasons for the faith that is within him, he unwittingly exposes the unbelief sheltered in his own bosom.

A mere negative attitude usually leads us to oppose every move of our fellow-believers that does not in every detail conform to our own viewpoint. We are prone to label as fanatic emotionalism any spiritual longings that do not correspond to our own limited experiences.

It is wrong to sneer at religious fervor even though it be a misdirected fervor. It is a mistake which we make so frequently. How much rather should we humbly and penitently confess that there is so very little of eager, contagious enthusiasm in our Christian life. "Would that all Jehovah's people were prophets, that Jehovah would put his Spirit upon them!"

Furthermore we have no license to dismiss such fervor with a gesture of superiority; still less to treat it as a joke. Sheep should be fed; not frightened. They know not what they do, who make light of that which concerns the eternal destiny of human souls. "And moreover a most excellent way I show unto you." We usually forget that the "excellent way" of love is pointed out as especially suitable in dealing with this problem. Let Christians profit by the experience of our fathers in dealing with fanaticism. Prohibitory measures have their use but it is limited. Surely history teaches us that persecution, whether by insinuation or by inquisition, only adds fuel to the fire.

We are to walk not as fools, but as wise. The days are evil. Demons and evil men make them so. It is no better to live in a fool's paradise than in a fanatic's paradise with respect to this problem. Irreparable losses have been suffered because of this inexcusable excuse that the situation was not serious. The situation is not trifling; it is sobering. Divine wisdom alone will avail.

If any man is called upon to deal with a religious movement, the Lord has not left him resourceless. Let him do as Solomon did, when called to shepherd Israel of old. Solomon first worshipped by bringing great sacrifices to the Lord. After having thus tuned his heart to commune with God he brings to remembrance Jehovah's faithfulness in the past, and confesses his own inability to govern the covenant nation. Whereupon he prays: "Give thy servant therefore an understanding heart to judge thy people, that I may discern between good and evil."

There is such a thing as spiritual insight. It is more than intelligence; it is what the Scriptures call discernment; not a *head* but a *heart* of wisdom. It is not the product of scholarship, though it will make use of both learning and experience. It is a God-given ability to understand and evaluate spiritual things. Not all disciples of Jesus possess this gift in the same measure, but all can prayerfully exercise the gift they have and ask God for more as they need it.

No one is appointed to lord it over the flock, but our Lord may expect us to lead men out of error. If any man lacketh wisdom, let him ask of God, who giveth liberally and upbraideth not. Then alone shall he be able to say, "Thanks be unto God, who always leadeth us in triumph in Christ."

The next essential in dealing effectively with religious

problems is to stand firmly on Scriptural ground. We are prone to forget what a great variety of people were reached by the Gospel even during the time of the apostles. We need to remind ourselves that the New Testament is fully capable of meeting all kinds of characters in all kinds of circumstances in every place and in every age.

Our battle is the same as that of the Christians in Antioch, in Ephesus, in Corinth, in Rome. The same flesh, the same lusts, the same pride are with us as were with them. But so also is the same Holy Spirit powerful through the same Word.

Let the situation be ever so baffling, the obstacles ever so great, the prospects ever so discouraging—there is one unfailing way out: "Whatsoever he saith unto you, do it." That "whatsoever" covers every case without exception. What He says, do just that! God will take care of the difficulty; but His help presupposes implicit obedience to Christ on our part.

Human reason, inclination, and experience are to be reckoned with, but they are not the important factors in mapping out the way. Whatsoever God says in His Word decides, be that ever so foolish in the opinion of men. Do that, and the Lord will be responsible for the outcome. Man's advice may be good, or it may be bad; God's command is always a safe rule.

There are at least two definite precepts in the Bible applying to pentecostalism; more specifically to one particular feature, the speaking in tongues. Those precepts are found in Paul's First Epistle to the Corinthians. That is where one would expect to find divine guidance with respect to this. For we know, Corinthian tongues had become a problem.

The first Biblical precept to be noticed is I Cor. 14:27-28. Brief reference was made to this in a previous chapter. Paul says: "If any man speaketh in a tongue, let it be by two, or at the most three, and that in turn; and let one interpret: but if there be no interpreter let him keep silence in the church."

Many who were on the verge of plunging into the whirlpool of tongue-talking have been kept from such a step by reading and re-reading the two Bible verses just quoted. Let any open minded man compare this clear command of Scripture with the procedure, the disorder in a typical pentecostal assembly. Then he may determine whether or not pentecostalism is under the judgment of God's Word.

One can scarcely conceive of a more open flaunting of Bible teaching. Instead of letting the tongue-talking "be by two, or at the most three," the practice seems to be the more, the merrier. Instead of speaking in turn, the rule is not to call for the floor, but to fall on the floor. This is not unkind exaggeration; it is the plain truth.

Again we say: let Christian men who are inclined toward pentecostalism read those two verses carefully and prayerfully. Not much comment is necessary when one takes his stand on the Bible.

The second Scriptural advice pertaining to this problem is found in I Cor. 14:39. "Desire earnestly to prophesy, and forbid not to speak with tongues." Already we have said of this word, that here we have divine psychology applied. Had Paul consulted one of us, we probably should have said as Joshua once said to Moses: "forbid them" (Num. 11:28). Stop this speaking in tongues!

The Holy Spirit did not direct the apostle unconditionally to forbid this practice in Corinth. And that which applies to Corinth, generally speaking applies elsewhere.

Perhaps we need to pause for prayer right here; prayer to yield gladly to the authority of the Word, even though it may run counter to our reasoning.

Surely it does occur to us at first sight that it would have been far simpler and wiser to prohibit the tongue-talking and be done with it. Did not the Holy Spirit know that this particular gift was misused in Corinth? Did He not know that it would become even a curse later in the Church? Did He not know that there would be an aftermath of wrecked lives wherever tongues appeared? Surely the Holy Spirit knew all this, and He knows it now. And yet He caused the apostle to write plainly: Forbid not!

Human comment, perhaps, can do little here. Often we hinder the Word by too much comment and enlargement. Still if we never lose sight of the authority of Scripture, we may benefit by sharing one another's views and reactions to such a statement.

"Forbid not" because man may not summarily condemn that which God has not so judged. A gift is not forthwith to be condemned because of misuse. If we presume to do that, we have stepped off from Scriptural ground and are in error.

"Forbid not" because many who covet the signs have not yet seen that it is a lust for vainglory. Direct their attention away from signs, and instead point to the Savior. Their holy ambition should be to have the same mind which was in Christ Jesus.

"Forbid not" because thereby you may drive many weak and unstable brethren into the very arms of those who profess to have understanding and sympathy. Some men have a martyr complex. Tell them that all things are lawful to a true believer, but all things are not expedient.

"Forbid not" lest they who are chronic spiritual invalids turn to religious quacks for treatment. There are folks who are "ever learning and never able to come to the knowledge of the truth." They enjoy ill health. Direct their attention away from self to Christ, who came to give life abundantly.

"Forbid not." It is sure to arouse the curiosity and desire of many, especially those who are attracted to that which is bizarre and sensational. Cause them to see the nobler, the holier challenge of love which is greater than to speak with the tongues of men or of angels. If there must be display, let it be not a burned body but a burning love.

"Forbid not" for in so doing you give occasion to those who habitually are "railing in matters whereof they are ignorant." They are false teachers, and they welcome opposition from anything orderly and established. They make capital of that which is forbidden, and become the heroes of malcontents and radicals.

"Forbid not," for thereby you advertise the wares of religious hucksters among men whose religious interest is chiefly negative. We are slow to learn that "legal deterrants are in their very nature irritants." If we keep a discreet silence, the opposition may spend itself in "beating the air." That gives opportunity for the Holy Spirit to convict of sin.

"Forbid not." Where the Spirit of the Lord is, there is liberty. By the grace of God you may be able to win those who in license "oppose themselves." It is worse than useless to rail at false teachers. They thrive on that. And it is equally futile to scold their followers. Disciples of Christ are not called to indulge in religious scolding. Calm self-possession will accomplish its end where censoriousness will fail. The very act of forbidding presupposes authority; and authority is prone to become despotic, not least in matters of religion.

The exhortation to encourage "prophesying" in preference to "tongues" is the conclusion of the entire three-chapter discussion on this problem. It is the apostle's "last word" on the subject. It has the emphasis of finality. The lesson to us is plain. We are not to encourage men to public tongue-talking. We are not even to make it an occasion for the flesh by forbidding it. Rather we are to discourage it by affording it no notoriety. On the other hand, we are to suggest the cultivation of another grace-gift instead.

Let "prophesying," the public testimony based on the Word, become more universal. Eliminate tongues, not by forbidding, but by pointing out a better way of being spent for Christ. There is no conceivable limit to the development and use of that most excellent way, the love which edifies the Church. Such love is not indulgent, but it is kind.

We believe it can not be emphasized too strongly that in dealing with this problem we must seek grace to be warm-hearted. We are too apt to be hot-headed, and if we are, our cause is defeated at the very outset.

We can do nothing against the truth. Surely we do not want to, even if it were possible. But we are not to champion the cause of truth merely for abstract truth's sake, but for the living truth, yea for Him who is true and is the Truth.

It is possible in a contest with error to win the debate but to lose the soul we would lead into the truth. A heated argument never kindles the Holy Spirit's fire in the heart. Therefore our motive must not only be sincere; it must be *obvious* that we are constrained by the love of Christ. If that is not plainly evident it matters little how eloquent or fervent or correct we are, the Holy Spirit can not use us. The motives, the attitude to the entire problem must always be a *compassionate* passion for souls.

THE ANSWER

No hopeless situations with God.

Power more important than program.

Speak all the words that I command thee.

Utilize all grace-gifts.

Contact men first for Christ.

Hearts on fire in Christ-like holiness.

Quench not the Spirit.

And he hath said unto me, My grace is sufficient for thee; for my power is made perfect in weakness. Most gladly therefore will I rather glory in my weaknesses, that the power of Christ may rest upon me (II Cor. 12:9).

Therefore saith the Lord, Jehovah of hosts, the Mighty One of Israel, Ah, I will ease me of mine adversaries, and avenge me of mine enemies; and I will turn my hand upon thee, and thoroughly purge away thy dross, and will take away all thy tin; and I will restore thy judges as at the first, and thy counsellors as at the beginning: afterward thou shalt be called The city of righteousness, a faithful town. Zion shall be redeemed with justice, and her converts with righteousness (Isaiah 1:24-27).

The mystery of the seven stars which thou sawest in my right hand, and the seven golden candlesticks. The seven stars are the angels of the seven churches: and the seven candlesticks are seven churches. To the angel in the church of Ephesus write: These things saith he that holdeth the seven stars in his right hand, he that walketh in the midst of the seven golden candlesticks: I know thy works, and thy toil and patience, and that thou canst not bear evil men, and didst try them that call themselves apostles, and they are not, and didst find them false; and thou hast patience and didst bear for my name's sake, and hast not grown weary. But I have this against thee, that thou didst leave thy first love. Remember therefore whence thou art fallen, and repent and do the first works; or else I come to thee, and will move thy candlestick out of its place, except thou repent. But this thou hast, that thou hatest the works of the Nicolaitans, which I also hate. He that hath an ear, let him hear what the Spirit saith to the churches. To him that overcometh, to him will I give to eat of the tree of life, which is in the Paradise of God (Rev. 1:20—2:7).

CHAPTER TEN

The Answer

NO problem is solved until it is solved right. No problem is even on its way to solution until its proportions are realized and its nature rightly understood.

Certain doctrines characterize nearly all pentecostal denominations. We have intentionally omitted the mention of most of them, as this is not a treatise on dogmas, but rather observations on the practical results of the doctrines involved. When we have found that the ailment is religious inflation, we know the cause is misconstrued or misapplied Bible passages. As in most cases, the error in doctrine is the primary evil but few are aware of that. It is therefore true as we stated in an early chapter, that the practical problem of pentecostalism among our people is an attitude, a phase of religious behaviour.

The external feature which is most puzzling and most vexing to evangelical believers is the "tongues." For that is the most alluring to so many. Nevertheless that is not the only error involved. This we have stated repeatedly, and this every reader can verify for himself.

The question then, that finally confronts us, is whether or not we can meet the situation. If we see the situation, if we have determined the approach, have we the remedy? Is there no balm in Gilead? Is there no physician there? What is the answer?

Yes, there is a remedy. We firmly believe that, and for many reasons. The Lord will not leave us stranded if this is a matter that concerns the welfare of His Church.

In this, as in every trying situation His Word points the way out and His promises support us. He has the remedy. The experience of God's people indicates how it may be applied.

It is not presumptuous to say this. If it were only the present writer's opinion, that might be true. But the Church may well trust His Word, who said: "Fear not, little flock!" The Church shall prevail, in spite of all the clever trickery of hell. The promise to each individual may well be applied to the group also, "There hath no temptation taken you but such as men can bear." Even Corinthian disciples were given that assurance. That which is a hopeless situation to us is not so to God. He is never at a loss what to do.

Not infrequently some saint of God is fearful that the Lord is about to withdraw the Shekinah of His presence from us. God *can* remove the candlestick. He has done so in ages past with other peoples. We deserve to be left with little light for we have so often placed it under a bushel. Still let us not by doubt and fears cause the Lord to leave us groping in darkness. Let us not open the way for the powers of darkness by our own unbelief.

The needs of our age are not new, no matter how much men insist they are. What others required we require. What has sufficed for others will suffice for us. The Holy Scriptures have never made men worldly wise but are still able to make us wise unto salvation. Therefore in this as in all else pertaining to Christian life and living it will be to us according to our faith.

Spiritual problems yield to spiritual treatment. Other methods fail. The educational, the social, the scientific methods have important places even in the program of the Church, but will never answer the purpose when the problem lies in a plane above the merely human and cultural.

The first answer to this question is that we *put power before program*. Not without program but as the more important of the two.

"All power is given unto me," our Lord announced before He said, "go ye, therefore." That power is our security; it is also our strength. "Ye shall receive power" is His promise to us. The power is neither men, nor money, nor mind, needful as these be. The Holy Spirit is the power. He alone supplies the oil whereby the light of the Church is kept burning bright.

At times the program of the Church has been form without fervor. Having a form of godliness but denying the power thereof. It was well said by a noted American preacher not long ago, "The progress of the Cross must not be hindered by bickerings about forms." We fear that some have stared so long at forms that they have forgotten the fire.

True it is that some people propose to stir up spiritual life by stirring up disorder, even a studied disorder. They forget that men may, and do, worship in a liturgical service. But that mistake is no worse than is theirs who proceed as if a rigidly correct form of service were the greatest essential of true worship. There is such a thing as being "faultily faultless" even in public worship. Men are prone to react to this in one of two ways; either to substitute a Jerusalem-worship or a Gerizim-worship for that which is in "spirit and in truth," or they will go to the other extreme "hitting the sawdust trail" in some "tabernacle" recently pitched across the street.

Are we too settled, too "correct"? Or is there a lack of red blood in the veins of the soldiers of the Cross? If the Church would be bold for Christ, she must bleed with Christ. If she would remain pure in faith, she must be passionate in love to her Bridegroom. And it must be said of her, as of her Lord, "Zeal for thy house shall eat me up." Christ was not "formal" when He cleansed the temple.

There is in our midst no little "religious emphasis" at occasions, but where is emphatic religion? The Christian life of some is dull and uninteresting because it lacks challenge. It is profession without experience. "They feel that their religion does not mean much to them—and it doesn't."

Now nothing is gained for the cause of Christ by being simply a "calamity howler," and no more is gained by taking the position of "peace at any price" when the price is compromise. In our warfare against error we need to turn to our Heavenly Father, coming daily with boldness to the throne of grace, that we may receive mercy and may find grace to help us in time of need. The air of materialism and frivolity surrounds us. We breathe that air. It is as poison gas. The power, the vitality which God's Spirit can give, alone is sufficient to withstand.

The day may have to come when men shall be compelled to distinguish between "religion" and Christianity. For sometimes the two are incompatible. The Apostle Paul found the cultured Athenians "very religious." Their very religiousness was what made them scoff at the Gospel of a risen Christ. The worldling must turn to Christ; so must the respectable churchling. Both need something more than a "moderate infusion of the religious element." They need the new life of faith in Jesus Christ.

How shall that power of which we speak manifest itself? In a correct doctrine correctly expressed? Mere form of worship and mere words of doctrine will not frighten the devil. Our language may be ever so exact, but as long as it is not translated into definite faith the powers of evil are not disturbed. "One little word" will overthrow the devil, if that word is from God; a thousand of our own big words are of no avail.

There can be no doubt but that the devil enjoys many an eloquent sermon. What travesties are committed in the name of preaching! Hungry souls can not feed on stones. Such diet has driven many a one into the camps of fanaticism. We may be quick to apply the words in Ezekiel 13:9 to the preacher in some radical cult, but we had better notice that Jehovah's judgment is upon the prophet, whose sin is saying "peace, and there is no peace." How watchful he must be who is preaching and teaching the Word, lest he too be found among those who seduce God's people! Where preachers tone down the call to repentance, conceal the Blood of cleansing, and offer hope outside of Christ, there all will be quiet—with the quietness of the grave.

Horatius Bonar points out in one of his writings that the "guarded gospel" may be no gospel at all. There is no backsliding in its wake because it never led to a going forward. Is it not better to arouse men, though some may again fall asleep, than to leave all in danger? Where the preaching does not penetrate there will be "few falling away because there was nothing to fall away from."

The purpose of preaching to the unconverted "is not to help the awakened soul to *evade* a personal decision, but to impel him to make a decision, and to help him to decide right."

Someone has said, "It takes four or more men to carry a dead human body, but one man carried that body alone up and down any flight of stairs *as long as his spirit dwelt in the body.*" The Church without the Holy Spirit's indwelling power is no church at all. It is a corpse. Probably very quiet, very peaceful, very beautifully dressed as by an undertaker, but a corpse just the same.

The Holy Spirit never exaggerates. He neither condones nor overstates our case but tells us the true state of affairs.

He does not point to ethics and ideals and aspirations until *after* He has introduced the Lamb of God.

"No preaching is great Christian preaching if it fails to convert men to Christ." Conversion is the one miracle that must be expected continually in the Church. The more fully and freely the old faith is proclaimed the more certain it is to produce saints as of old. Such preaching may not always fill the auditorium of the church but it has Christ's own promise that it shall fill heaven. As it is futile to use mere human remedies in dealing with sensationalism, so it is fatal to dilute the "spiritual milk which is without guile" in ministering to souls. Let Christian men cultivate and value culture and art, hygiene and psychiatry. Yet these will never do as a substitute for the Gospel of the Cross. Change of scenery and of diet may be useful but cannot take the place of a changed heart.

In the final analysis it makes little difference whether the Word is hid by the philosophy of a humanist or by the phantasies of a pentecostalist. In either case the Holy Spirit's work is prevented for He works through the Word.

We do well to heed the entire Word, "knowing this first that no prophecy of Scripture is of private interpretation." Not "private" so as to conform to our own favorite notions, nor so as to be interpreted independently of the rest of the Bible. Such "private interpretation" causes the lamp to become a mirage. *Formalism is as deadly as fanaticism.* Though some folks are constantly in a spiritual stew, they are no worse off than others who are kept in a spiritual refrigerator. Both end in death.

But suppose we fail, what then? Suppose we have contended valiantly for the truth and have consistently opposed error, and still our brethren leave and "walk no more with us," what then?

Then remember the Master's words, "A servant is no

greater than his lord." He had a large following for a short while. But when He spoke the searching truth the multitude left. Even the seventy disciples walked no more with Him. All He had left of His congregation was the twelve charter members. Christ asked them, "Would ye also go away?"

Suppose that Peter's answer had been: "Master, we prefer to remain, but we suggest that you modify your gospel somewhat. The people do not like your direct applications. It effects the attendance, and we fear the treasury will suffer; in fact Judas, the treasurer, complains now." Would such reasoning have swerved Christ from the way of obedience? Would not He have said as He did later, when urged to compromise, "Get thee behind me, Satan?" According to standards of men, even men who once had served Him, Christ was a failure.

Again, in the words of Dr. Hallesby we would say: "It is by no means my intention to say that clear and precise argumentation on the part of the preacher will result in the awakening and conversion of his listeners. By no means. Both awakening and conversion come as the result of the sinner coming into contact with the supernatural powers of salvation which emanate to him from Christ through the Word."

"But inasmuch as the Word of Christ is the means through which the supernatural work of the Spirit is accomplished, it is important that we preach this Word in all its fulness and that we rightly divide the Word of God."

"Not failure, but low aim, is crime," be it in the pulpit or in the pew. That which appears to be a failure may be delayed victory. An army is not defeated though one sector is checked. Battles are won through such reverses. "Our greatest triumph is not in never falling, but in rising every time we fall." You may be tempted to do as Elijah once did; he ran away and laid down under a juniper bush and wanted to die. The Great Physician understood. He let him rest a while, let him learn a much needed lesson on gentleness, and then sent him back to the wayward people.

Once Elisha's servant lost courage. He cried, "Alas my master how shall we do!" The answer was, "Fear not, for they that are with us are more than they that are with them."

"There is no restraint to Jehovah to save by many or by few." "Thou, therefore, gird up thy loins and arise, and speak unto them all that I have commanded thee: be not dismayed at them, lest I dismay thee before them." "I have made thee a trier and a fortress among my people, that thou mayest know and try their way." "Speak all the words that I command thee to speak unto them; diminish not a word. It may be they will hearken and turn every man from his evil way." "How canst thou be quiet, seeing Jehovah hath given thee a charge?"

"But if the watchman . . . blow not the trumpet, and the people be not warned, and the sword come and take away any person from among them . . . his blood will I require at the watchman's hand. . . Nevertheless if thou warn the wicked . . . thou hast delivered thy soul."

When called upon to meet the onslaught of false teaching and godless living, we must confess, "We have no might against this great company that cometh against us, neither know we what to do: but our eyes are upon thee." Then will the Lord of hosts assure us, "The battle is not yours but God's. Ye shall not need to fight in this battle; set yourselves, stand ye still and see the salvation of Jehovah with you, O Judah and Jerusalem."

The second answer to this question is: the Church must set about seriously to *utilize all the grace-gifts* which the Lord has given to her.

God has bountifully given gifts to the Church. "He gave some to be apostles; and some, prophets; and some, evangelists; and some, pastors and teachers; for the perfecting of the saints, unto the work of ministering, unto the building up of the body of Christ." These gifts are chiefly those needed in the founding of the Church, but those necessary for the continuation of the spread of the Word are also included.

However, the Lord never intended that all service should be left to those who preach and teach. There are also other "men of good report, full of the Spirit and of wisdom" in the congregation. There are diversities of gifts, but the same Spirit. And there are diversities of ministrations, and the same Lord. And there are diversities of workings, but the same God who worketh all things in all. But to each one is given the manifestation of the Spirit to profit withal.

These gifts are not given that some may be extolled and others buried in the ground. That was precisely what caused near-havoc in Corinth. Their catering to the more spectacular powers made them unbalanced.

"Helps" and "governments" (I Cor. 12:28) are the Lord's gifts to a church as truly as are pastors and teachers. And it takes much grace to be known simply as a "help" and nothing more. Also, it requires divine wisdom and love to be in the executive position of "government" in a church, if the service shall redound to the glory of Christ alone. It would not be amiss for the pastor, the moderator, the presiding officer of the church council, the chairman of the Board of Trustees, and others in like positions, to read III John 9-10, of "Diotrephes who loveth to have the preeminence among them . . . prating against us with wicked words . . . and casteth (others) out of the church."

Not all shall lead; that leads nowhere. Christ has set

some to be elders to direct and watch over His people. However, He never limited the bearing of public testimony in the assembly to the elders alone. Men have frequently presumed to pass such ordinances, but without the Lord's approval.

At a distinct loss we have frequently divorced the spiritual from the practical in our discipleship. It has led to an unfortunate placement of forces within the congregation. We seem to agree that the deacon should be a man of piety; but as for the church trustee, we act as if we prefer one "not too religious." The "testimony" at many a mid-week meeting does not much disturb the sinner; it does sometimes vex the saint. It does not always magnify the Name of Christ. And when we call at the home of a grief-stricken neighbor we probably speak of all else except Him who alone can give rest to the weary soul.

If such a situation obtains—and we all know it does—the charge must be laid largely to an unused, untrained, unconsecrated membership within the congregation.

If gifts are found in the congregation let them be set to work. Exercise the faith in faithfulness and it will increase, for God expects men to stir up the gifts within them. There are no defects in the divine Word, no scantiness of divine grace, no want of opportunity to bear witness. "Ye shall receive power, and ye shall be my witnesses."

It is a pity that "bickering about forms" has more than once given an opening to the enemy. The Lord's army has been "too well disciplined" to dare anything. An army is orderly; but it is not made up of order; it is made up of men; not officers only, but privates as well. We shall have a carnal, a weak Church, if we fail to mobilize *all* Christian man-power for Christ. Unused equipment deteriorates. Unused graces are lost. If we, instead of in honor preferring one another, ignore others so as to make vay for our own prestige, we need not wonder that sects seem inviting to our people.

No army ever advanced by being only on the defensive. Neither can the Church. Soldiers of Christ, arise, not only to drive out error but also to establish the truth! If nothing is supplied to replace the evil driven out, then will it soon return to the "swept and garnished," but unoccupied house, and a multiplied host of wickedness will take possession. It is so in the heart of the individual; it is so in the assembly of believers.

Not that modern church folk are not kept busy. Not that at all. But our busyness has not *spiritual* values as its chief objective. Therefore it really gets us nowhere. Someone has called churches "beehives of activity, with more hum than honey." May God forgive us! We fear that the Keeper-of-the-bees gets a sting more often than honey from the hives. One can hardly escape the conviction that the endless list of clubs, circles, conferences, conventions,—ad infinitum—has given the Church the regimentation of a CCC camp. And to that extent curbed the initiative which is of the Holy Spirit. Organization is necessary, but it never supplies power. Order is Scriptural, but it is not to supplant life.

> "Dear Lord and Father of mankind,
>   Forgive our feverish ways;
>   Reclothe us in our rightful mind,
>   In purer lives Thy service find,
>   In deeper reverence praise.
>   Drop Thy still dews of quietness
>   Till all our strivings cease;
>   Take from our souls the strain and stress,
>   And let our ordered lives confess
>   The beauty of Thy peace."

At the risk of being charged with "other-worldliness" we raise the question whether the Church of Jesus Christ ever was called to "build a better world" as that phrase is usually understood. Such a building program is taken to be an invitation to "do things" for the Lord. But its method and spirit usually demotes Christ from being a Savior to being a mere helper. Christ did not live and die to "help" the world; He came to *save* it.

Salvation is man's urgent need. All else is secondary, and even futile where Christ is pushed into the background. When the Greeks came to the Jewish disciples they came not for a program. They would see Jesus. When Europe called to Asia to "come over and help," it did not need help in human culture such as Asia had to offer. The Macedonian cry was for peace with God!

If and when church committees and clubs make it their definite practise to contact men first for Christ, they will have a hold on the hearts, with which no social ties can be compared. When missionary plans and surveys distinctly call for Christ-membership as more important than church-membership, we shall have a "re-thinking missions" that shall enlist the best for the work at home and abroad.

Of course humans are never able to separate the wheat and the tares. To attempt that only leads into other errors. But we may, and must exercise a holy vigilance over our hearts and our churches. For we are distinctly called to "come out and be separate" from the worldliness of the world.

Some people lean toward an academic religion as though Christ were an abstract idea; others incline to emotional experience as if Christianity were a touching ballad. God gave men intellect but not that they might turn it into an idol; He also gives men fervent feelings, but not that these shall supplant faith.

It is still true that the deep things of the Spirit may be hid from the wise and the prudent, and be revealed unto babes. The less intellectual also have a place to fill, and it is not an unimportant place. Perchance "their faith is not weakened by disproportioned culture of reason," and they may have a firmer grip upon the deep spiritual realities of the faith.

We have pointed out that if they are wrong who believe that such an ability as speaking in tongues is proof of spiritual unction, they are just as sadly in error who persist in refusing to utilize the grace-gifts. Let the Church discover, cultivate, and employ all such gifts, and there will be small entrance for cults. Let the Church *definitely encourage and train its entire membership continually to bear public witness for Christ in word and in deed* and there will not be much danger of spiritual anarchy and sensationalism. Healthy spiritual life goes before active social life; a life that is not suppressed but expressed by laity as much as by clergy.

Where the Holy Spirit rules unhindered there is liberty; not anarchy, and not bondage. He does not produce mimics, nor misfits, nor artificial characters. When such appear, as they sometimes do, the Lord did not call them out to where they find themselves. They are on the wrong shelf, either because of their own wilful choice, or because someone else maneuvered their decision. The enlisting of all believers, men and women, learned and unlearned, will be found to produce vigor and balance in the life of the congregation.

Perhaps someone who reads this will insist that ministers denounce pentecostalism because of bigotry and are opposed to a layman's testimony in the congregation because of jealousy.

Is there much truth in such a charge? We know that pastors are not exempt from temptation. Satan will assail the shepherd more fiercely than he does the sheep. Nevertheless let us beware lest we thoughtlessly bring charges against the ministers. The accusations may be unwarranted, wicked. They frequently are.

Many a pastor has been weighed down in agony over the unconverted members of his flock, and yet more crushed in disappointment over the attitude of those who profess to believe.

We know of not a few young men who in their zeal were ready to welcome any traveling "brother" that happened along. Soon they discovered that the "missionary" was not so much bent on bringing souls to Christ as he was to "talk up a new tabernacle." The "message" would be a ranting against the "dead preachers," and the exhortation toward a "new baptism." In short, the church was not being revived but wrecked.

After a few such bitter experiences it is not strange that the minister questions and even opposes many a peddler of religion. Surely it is but his pastoral duty to warn against wolves in sheep's clothing.

If we want a spiritual quickening in our midst, let us not prepare for it by denouncing the pastor. We shall wait in vain if we do. "Touch not mine anointed ones and do my prophets no harm" is a word directed to those of us who occupy the pew. The Lord has never granted indulgence to transgress against that word.

The same Lord who has given gifts to the Church and who would have them used, will also strengthen and reward each one. It is the law of life that each shall be recognized by the Lord for service rendered. "If any man's work shall abide . . . he shall receive a reward." "What soldier ever serveth at his own charges?" "Whatsoever is right" the Lord of the vineyard will surely give.

The law of equality laid down by the Lord is, "For as his share is that goeth down to the battle, so shall his share be that tarrieth by the baggage; they shall share alike." That is divine economics which makes for joy and contentment of brethren in the service.

"I beseech you therefore, brethren, by the mercies of God, to present your bodies a living sacrifice, holy, acceptable to God, which is your spiritual service. And be not fashioned according to this world; but be ye transformed by the renewing of your mind, that ye may prove what is the good and acceptable and perfect will of God. For I say through the grace that was given me, to every man that is among you, not to think of himself more highly than he ought to think; but so to think as to think soberly, according as God hath dealt to each man a measure of faith. For even as we have many members in one body, and all members have not the same office; so we, who are many, are one body in Christ, and severally members, one of another" (Rom. 12:1-5).

Our first answer as to the remedy was that we recognize spiritual power to be a greater need than program and that formalism is no better than fanaticism. The second answer was that all disciples be used, and encouraged to confess Christ in the assembly of believers, and to bear public testimony both in addressing men and in serving men.

We venture the third answer: *hearts on fire in a Christ-like holiness.* Surely this last is not the least.

When the Israelites wanted to continue leading unholy lives without quite cutting themselves off from the care of Jehovah, they based their hopes on the temple. As long as the sanctuary was in their midst they were in carnal security. Did not God then dwell amongst them, and were not the offerings of bullocks and the burning of incense a daily practise in the congregation? Did they not point with pride to the marble and the gold on Mount Moriah, saying: "The temple of Jehovah, the temple of

Jehovah, the temple of Jehovah are these"? But the prophet says they trusted in lying words.

Whenever men today "keep up the church" in the hopes God shall then overlook their unholy living, they follow in the train of the Israelites of old. More than that, they need to remind themselves that purity of doctrine grants no indulgence for impurity of life.

"Holiness" groups have sprung up in the Church down through the ages. Before long such movements nearly always found themselves much the same as those from whom they separated, so far as their "holiness" was concerned. But *why did such movements arise?* In nearly every instance it was a protest, a struggle against the worldliness of Christians.

Is it not true that when we hear of "holiness people" we are prone to dismiss the matter with a feeling of smug satisfaction that "at least we are not holy"? What an awful thought! What fearful judgement we pronounce upon ourselves when we take such a stand!

In avoiding the error of teaching sinlessness, we have gone to the opposite extreme and have neglected a life of holiness. In order to keep ourselves from becoming "holy jumpers" we have permitted ourselves to walk in the counsel of the wicked. There are no tears in heaven. If there were, then surely the Savior who shed His blood to save us would shed His tears because of our walk. Alas, we do grieve the Holy Spirit, the Spirit of Christ in our midst.

If we say we have no sin we deceive ourselves. If we live in sin that grace may abound we also deceive ourselves. The "sinless perfection" of certain sectarians is not the "holiness without which no man shall see the Lord." The two teachings are not the same. The one is a deception, the other is the "high calling of God in Christ Jesus." Even the Spirit-filled apostle Paul had not yet attained nor was yet made perfect, but he did stretch forward to get nearer and still nearer to that goal. We, unlike him, permit ourselves to drift along idly and indifferently.

"Like as he who called you is holy, be ye yourselves also holy in all manner of living; because it is written, Ye shall be holy; for I am holy. And if ye call on him as Father, who without respect of persons judgeth according to each man's work, pass the time of your sojourning in fear." That is God's standard of holiness for anyone who says, "Our Father who art in heaven." It is His standard, not only with respect to our being holy with an imputed holiness in justification, and the holiness of being set apart for God's service; *it is also a holiness which is revealed in the righteousness of life.*

The Father is also the impartial Judge. He will forgive sin, but never excuse it. He is not indulgent even toward His children, though He pities them that fear Him. "Let every one that nameth the name of the Lord depart from unrighteousness." Otherwise he will be a useless vessel in the Church. There will never be much power in our testimonies as long as we are satisfied with a minimum of the Holy Spirit's grace. As with the Church, so with each member: he must *glow* in order to grow; fervent, burning, in spirit serving the Lord.

All fulness dwells in Christ, and He has made ample provision for our being made like unto Himself. He calls us to that likeness. As He was sent into the world, even so does He send us, every disciple, into the world. Our responsibility to follow Him is great but not greater than the means provided for its attainment.

Christian church members frequently deplore the spiritual condition of a neighbor sitting next to them in the pew. They vaguely hope that the pastor's handshake at the door shall somehow excuse their own reluctance to speak to the unsaved. To be sure they are quite ready to invite the unbeliever to the guild or the club, but not to invite him to Christ. That is not "good form."

When we read of Nehemiah's concern for his countrymen it puts us to shame. He was not a priest nor a prophet; he was layman in a high position, a statesman. He wept over the plight of God's Israel. Was he effeminate, or did he shed manly tears? It means something when a strong man weeps. It ought to mean much if he weeps over the lost! Nehemiah did not say, "I feared that; I had no faith in such a going back to the Holy Land; Babylon is good enough for me." No, he mourned over the weak and discouraged brethren in Jerusalem. He confessed their sins as if they were his own—and then he petitioned the king for help. What kind of help? He would go, and do what he could for them. More Nehemiahs among our laymen; then more power and progress for God's people.

In the latter days false prophets shall be popular, and as for others "the love of many shall wax cold." Are we among them? "Lord, is it I?" At that very time when the disciples asked that question, we are told that Jesus "having loved his own that were in the world, he loved them unto the end." Is it because there is so little in us of that mind which was in Christ Jesus that the bewildered and burdened souls leave us and turn to false prophets?

"When the Lord turns the Captivity of Zion" how do we take it? Are our mouths filled with the laughter of holy joy? Or has it been the laughter of derision? God forbid! When men have come for spiritual aid, have we told them "not to give way to emotions," "to leave off worrying about such things," that they were "all right"? Are men "all right" who have no peace with God?

The abundant life in Christ is not imaginary or utopian. It is a reality to be experienced, because Christ gives it

to men. Life outside of Christ may appear ruddy and
vigorous and still the appearance be only the effect of religious cosmetics. It may throb with energy due only to a
dangerous stimulant. The heart may be warm, the eye
bright, and the tongue loosed because of fever instead of
faith.

Quench not the Spirit if He is present to work. He
will not speak of mere conformity to church rule; He will
not lead to the extravagances of mere emotion; He will
re-create men and transform them into the image of the
Lord from glory to glory. He will teach us all that true
holiness is active, but that it does not spring from activity.
Christ enthroned is the source. The Spirit-filled disciple
is the most humble, yet the most bold. In his own eyes
he is "less than the least." His life is Spirit-filled because
it is *Christ-filled.*

In our warfare against the errors of men and the wiles
of the devil we are not left to our own resources. Nor
need we depend on our own strength for a closer walk
with God. The dew of daily grace will descend upon us
if we but look to Jesus. Nay, more, "the river of God is
full of water." It is a fountain for our quickening as well
as for our cleansing. It is "a well of water springing up
unto eternal life"; and from within each one who drinks
freely "shall flow rivers of living water."

What a comfort and what assurance to know that He
who knows our frame and loves us unto the end distributes
His gifts according to His own will, and bestows on each
that which shall profit all. Thanks be unto Him for the
Church and for every grace bestowed on its members.
May He never find occasion to rebuke us as once He
rebuked His people of old: "Except ye see signs and
wonders ye will not believe."

"The firm foundation of God standeth, having this seal:
The Lord knoweth them that are his; and, Let everyone

that nameth the Name of the Lord depart from unrighteousness. In a great house there are many vessels, some unto honor, and some unto dishonor." If a man therefore purge himself from these—who concerning the truth have erred—he shall be a vessel unto honor, sanctified. meet for the Master's use, prepared unto every good work.

Faith, resting on that foundation, has feeling, a feeling that is more than the thrill of adventure, and which is beyond the fret of nerves. It is quiet confidence. God gave us not a spirit of fearfulness, but of power and love and discipline. And He gave us a faith that will trust and obey; that can truly say, "though he slay me, yet will I trust him," and though at times it be a tearful obedience, it nevertheless obeys.

Quench not the Spirit. Permit Him to use the gifts for the building up of the Church. No shouts of applause will be heard from the by-standers. No ecstasy will be the lot of those who walk this way for it is the way of the Cross. But they who launch out on that venture of faith, the venture of a daily decreasing of self that there may be room for a daily increasing of Christ, shall find that God is able to make all grace abound unto them. They will understand from daily experience, Paul's incomparable description of the Christian life when he says: "I have been crucified with Christ; and it is no longer I that live, but Christ liveth in me; and that life which I now live in the flesh I live in faith, the faith which is in the Son of God, who loved me, and gave himself up for me." That is the life abundant.

[3]